Martin of Tours

1 Much restored stained glass of 1220 in the north-east transept of Canterbury Cathedral over St Martin's altar, showing the saint, as a soldier in the Roman army, dividing his cloak with the beggar outside Amiens.

Martin of Tours

Parish Priest, Mystic and Exorcist

Christopher Donaldson

Routledge & Kegan Paul
London and Henley

First published in 1980
by Routledge & Kegan Paul Ltd
39 Store Street, London WC1E 7DD and
Broadway House, Newtown Road,
Henley-on-Thames, Oxon RG9 1EN
Set in 11 on 12 pt Garamond
and printed in Great Britain by
Ebenezer Baylis and Son Ltd
The Trinity Press, Worcester, and London
© Christopher Donaldson 1980

British Library Cataloguing in Publication Data

Donaldson, Christopher

Martin of Tours.
1. Martin of Tours, Saint
2. Christian saints – France – Tours – Biography
3. Tours – Biography
270.2'092'4   BR1720.M3

ISBN 0 7100 0422 2

Contents

Illustrations

Preface

Anyone who has cause to study the history of the fourth century of our era, must immediately be struck by the unique sense of rapport that exists between that century and ours. Many intelligent people living in the fourth century had the same overpowering feeling with which we are familiar, that they had arrived at a point where major and dramatic changes were about to take place in the whole order of things. On the one hand they were conscious of standing firmly rooted in a centuries old culture and tradition, yet on the other they were becoming more and more aware that their feet were on the threshold of a new age, an age in which practically every familiar landmark, physical, moral and spiritual was about to be swept away.

With this sense of dramatic change, the name of Christianity was intimately linked, and indeed was to provide the main formative influence in the centuries that lay ahead. As yet, however, the full implications of the peace of the church and the establishment of Christianity as the official state religion, had not made themselves fully felt; and these few decades in which the Christian church had found a new security and widespread popular acclaim, whilst still remaining a minority, were the vintage years of Christianity, to which the historical churches have always looked for norms of faith and spirituality.

Today in an increasingly secular and even hostile world, the Christian churches are once again freeing themselves from the shackles of heavy involvement in affairs of state and are seeking to find refreshment and encouragement from the spirituality of the primitive churches of the first four centuries; and it is not without significance that Martin, whose life spanned the fourth century, had a powerful influence on the spiritual formation of the late pope John XXIII, whose short tenure of the papal chair has had so much to do with the re-formation of modern church life in all the Churches.

I have written this book in the hope that it will arouse in many the same kind of recognition that I found in the researching and writing of it; for in a most mysterious way I found the message coming across to me from the fourth century to be highly relevant to our contemporary situation, both in church and society at large.

I do not lay claim to be a professional historian, for the historian's art is a complex and profound one that needs years of close study to perfect. I, on the other hand, have approached the study after thirty or more years of practice of the equally difficult yet satisfying art of being a parish priest; and knowledge of this arcane art has opened for me secrets that otherwise might not have been noted by the academic historian, for Martin was pre-eminently a skilled and capable parish priest.

Timothy Severin in his recently published *Voyage of Brendan* (Hutchinson, 1978) has shown vividly how such practical first-hand experience of another discipline can often provide the key to unlock the meaning of ancient texts, where he writes of the extraordinary voyage of himself and his companions in a leather boat through the ice floes of the North Atlantic:

> In the first place, the flavour of the mediaeval text now seems wholly authentic, when judged against our experiences aboard *Brendan*. The author of the (8th century) *Navigatio* obviously knew – as we now know – what it was like to be in an ocean-going curragh. He knew that it was impossible to row upwind in a boat which sits so high in the water that a foul wind blows you down on a hostile shore, however much you want to get clear ... we expected to regrease *Brendan* as we eventually did in Iceland, but without the spare oxhides to rig as a wave deflector off East Greenland, we could well have been swamped and foundered. Perhaps the moral of the tale is that every detail on practical matters in a mediaeval text ought to be noted, however trivial it might appear.

In much the same way I, as an experienced parish priest, could often recognize through the quaintness of Sulpitius' descriptions, the authenticity of Martin's pastoral experience and thrill to his sure touch.

The exploration of primitive Christianity in Britain described in chapter 15, sparked off by thirteen years of intimate association with the Roman tiles and stones of St Martin's church at Canterbury has been sheer delight. As I read or travelled the Roman roads of Britain on my motor cycle from Dover to Hadrian's wall and Ninian's cave in Galloway, and again down the Fosse Way to the rich Roman

Dorset and Devon country, I felt that even as I went along I was making new discoveries which could well spark off a kind of mass search for detailed information about the roots of our culture in which the most ordinary British citizen or foreign traveller could join and make significant contributions.

The connection between the sites of many ancient parish churches with Romano-Celtic pagan shrines or subsequent primitive Celtic buildings seems to be far closer than was ever thought, and much detailed work is waiting to be done in this area. For the powerful formative influence of the Celtic monks and hermits on English Christianity is only just beginning to be understood and the study of Martin will surely help us to grasp the profound significance of that small island where his cross still stands, and of which Sir Kenneth Clark's insight is so true:

> I never come to Iona – and I used to come here almost every year when I was young – without the feeling that 'some God is in this place'. It isn't as awe inspiring as some other holy places – Delphi or Assisi. But Iona gives one more than anywhere else I know a sense of peace and inner freedom. What does it? The light which floods round on every side? The lie of the land which, coming after the solemn hills of Mull, seems strangely like Greece, like Delos even? The combination of wine-dark sea, white sand and pink granite? Or is it the memory of those holy men who for two centuries kept western civilization alive? (*Civilization*, BBC and John Murray, 1969)

Many have helped me in the writing of the book, and I would wish to thank them all, but especially Mr Timothy O'Sullivan, whose valued advice and encouragement have taught me much; Dom Georges Lefèbvre and the Members of the Benedictine Community at Ligugé, for the use of their extensive library, for their kind hospitality and for their patience with my pidgin French; the Rev. Anthony Harvey, then Warden of St Augustine's College, Canterbury; Father Herbert Slade of the Society of St John the Evangelist and Archdeacon Bernard Pawley who read through the original draft and gave much encouragement; Sir Richard Southern, President of St John's College, Oxford; Canon J. Sadoux, Rector of the Basilica at Tours, with whom I exchanged visits and from whom I received much advice and help; the many librarians who have brought out of their treasures things new and old; and those two clergy of the American Episcopal Church, the Revs Ira Crowther and Harwood C. Bowman jnr, who encouraged me first to write the book, and gave me the title.

My only possible way of expressing my gratitude to Margaret, my wife, is to say that without her practical encouragement, the whole idea of writing the book would have been quite out of the question.

Christopher Donaldson
Horn Ash, Dorset

Acknowledgments

I wish to acknowledge my indebtedness to the work of Professeur Jacques Fontaine of the Sorbonne, whose definitive work, nos 133–5, in the series, Sources Chrétiennes, was placed in my hands by the librarian of the Benedictine community at Ligugé, on my arrival at their house to study the life of St Martin. The work, entitled, *Sulpice Sévère, Vie de St. Martin*, is in three volumes and was published in Paris by Les Editions du Cerf, in 1969. Reading through these volumes each day, I came to realize how much Professeur Fontaine had come to be my guide and encourager in my studies. His work must surely remain for all time a *sine qua non* for all who wish to explore the exciting world of Saint Martin and his times.

The author and publishers would also like to thank the following: Dom Jean Coquet, for permission to reproduce the plan of the excavations at Ligugé from *L'Intérêt de fouilles de Ligugé,* Société des amis des vieux Ligugé, 1968; Faber and Faber Ltd and Harcourt Brace Jovanovich Inc., for permission to reprint lines from 'Little Gidding' in *Four Quartets* by T. S. Eliot, copyright 1943 by T. S. Eliot, copyright 1971 by Esme Valerie Eliot; Niedersächsische Staats- und Universitätsbibliothek Göttingen, for permission to reproduce the illustration on p. 26 from cod. Ms. theol. 231, fol. 113ᵛ.

Chronological Table

DATE	LIFE OF MARTIN	POPE	EMPERORS	OTHER EVENTS
304		Marcellinus. Died in his bed at the height of the persecution.	Diocletian Augustus. Maximinian Augustus. Constantius I Caesar. Galerius Caesar.	Diocletian retires to Split at the height of the persecution.
305		Vacant for four years.	Severus and Maximinus Daia Caesars.	Diocletian and Maximian abdicate.
306			Galerius Augustus.	Constantius I dies at York. July, Constantine acclaimed as Augustus by the troops in Britain.
308		Marcellus elected.	Severus commits suicide.	
310		Marcellus banished. Eusebius elected and banished.	Licinius Augustus. Maximinus Augustus.	
311		Miltiades elected.		Galerius in sickness issues an edict of toleration of Christianity.
312				Maxentius, son of Maximinian, upstart Augustus at Rome, defeated at the battle of the Milvian Bridge, 28 October 312, by Constantine. The vision of the sign in the sky.

Year	Martin	Empire	Church offices	Christianity
313		Maximinus Daia commits suicide. Licinius Augustus. Constantine Augustus.		Edict of Milan. Toleration of Christianity; special favours for Christians.
314			Silvester elected.	War between two Augusti. COUNCIL OF ARLES, summoned by Constantine.
316	Martin born at Sabaria in Pannonia.			
319	Martin's parents move to Ticinum, Pavia, twenty miles from Milan.			Private practice of *haruspices* and sacrificial feasts in the home forbidden. Licinius begins persecution of Christians in the East again. The presbyter Arius disturbs the peace in Alexandria.
323		Licinius executed in Salonika. Constantine sole emperor.		Licinius defeated at Adrianople and Chrysopolis.
325				Constantine summons the COUNCIL OF NICAEA.
326	Martin enrols as catechumen aged ten.			Murder of Crispus, Constantine's eldest son. Murder of Fausta, Constantine's wife. Constantine with his mother Helena building basilicas.
328				Constantine recalls Arius and other deposed Arian bishops. Arianism makes strong progress. Bishop Alexander dies. Athanasius succeeds him.

DATE	LIFE OF MARTIN	POPE	EMPERORS	OTHER EVENTS
330				Constantine dedicates Constantinople.
331	Martin aged fifteen is forcibly enrolled in the army.			Edict of Constantine against all heretics forbidding their assemblies and confiscating their places of worship.
334	Martin aged twenty has vision of Christ wearing his military cloak.			Ausonius sets up his school of rhetoric at Bordeaux.
335				Synod of Tyre, hostile to Athanasius, Arius is banished by Constantine.
336				Arius dies.
337		Julius elected.	Sons of Constantine: Constantine II, aged twenty-one, Augustus; Constantius II, aged twenty, Augustus.	Constantine baptized on his death bed by the Arian bishop Eusebius of Nicomedia. Athanasius re-enters Alexandria.
338			Constans Augustus.	Meeting of three brothers at Viminiacum to divide the empire.
339				Athanasius leaves Alexandria, another bishop Gregory having been appointed in his place. Stays at Rome and speaks of Antony, and the monastic movement.
340				Constantine II dies fighting at Aquileia.
341				COUNCIL OF THE DEDICATION at Antioch conciliatory, semi-Arian.

342			Visit of semi-Arian bishops to Constans with form of Dedication creed.
343			COUNCIL OF SARDICA. Half western bishops half eastern; desire to issue a new creed; conflict over *homoousion*.
344			Attempts at reconciliation fail.
345			Gregory dies; Athanasius restored to Alexandria.
346			Pachomius dies in the desert.
350		Usurper Magnentius proclaimed. Constans assassinated.	Hilary renounces paganism and is baptized.
351			Battle of Mursa. Defeat of Magnentius. Constantius II makes his headquarters at Sirmium.
352	Liberius elected.		Constantius determined to force a form of semi-Arianism on the church and wages crusade against Athanasius and the Nicene creed. Serious invasions of Germans led by Chondomar.
353	Constantius exiles Liberius and appoints the archdeacon Felix to succeed him.		Hilary elected bishop of Poitiers. Paulinus of Nola born.

DATE	LIFE OF MARTIN	POPE	EMPERORS	OTHER EVENTS
354		Felix rejected by the people as pope.		Augustine born. Constantius decrees Christmas day to be held on 25 December.
355			Julian appointed Caesar to lead campaign in Gaul. His success.	Council held at pope's request at Milan. Bishops forced to sign Arian creed by Constantius or face exile. Lucifer of Calaris, Eusebius of Vercellae, Dionysius of Milan, Hilary of Poitiers, Rhodianus of Toulouse, pope Liberius – condemned to exile. The great invasion of the Germans grows in intensity and they reach as far as Autun.
356	Martin aged forty serving in the army at Worms under Julian, leaves and goes to join Hilary at Poitiers. Sets out for Pannonia to see his parents and try to convert them.			Bishop Hosius refuses to sign the new creed and is kept in custody at Sirmium. Athanasius, threatened, flees to the desert where he is looked after by the monks and writes the *Life of St Antony*, who has just died.
357	Martin leaves his parents and sets out for the 'city' (Sirmium?) to proclaim the Nicene faith.			Battle of Strasbourg. Complete victory for Julian. Constantius visits Rome and orders removal of statue of Liberty. Ursacius and Valens, Arian bishops, lead Arian campaign successfully. Liberius weakens and signs against Athanasius. Hosius weakens and signs Arian creed. Declaration of Arian faith signed by many bishops at SIRMIUM.

358	Martin sets up his cell at Milan, whence he is eventually driven by bishop Auxentius.		Athanasius publishes the *Life of St Antony*.
359	Sets up hermitage on the island of Gallinaria accompanied by a presbyter.		COUNCIL OF ARIMINUM (Rimini); 400 bishops assemble: 320 for Nicene faith, 80 Arians. Kept waiting seven months and eventually agree to sign the formulary, avoiding *homoousion*. COUNCIL AT SELEUCIA in the East. 150 eastern bishops forced to sign.
360		Liberius. Julian Caesar.	February COUNCIL OF CONSTANTINOPLE; delegates sign the Arian-style creed of Ariminum: 'the world groaned, and was astonished to find itself Arian'. Delegates attend dedication of St Sophia at Constantinople. Hilary in exile in Constantinople writes open letter 'Contra Constantium imperatorem'. April, Julian taken by his troops and crowned Augustus.
361	Martin arrives at Ligugé to found his first community.	Julian Augustus.	Hilary sent home to Poitiers. Julian marches towards Constantius at Antioch. November, Constantius dies. Julian enters Constantinople in December.
362			Hilary returns home. Julian actively reintroducing paganism and withdrawing all patronage from the clergy. He refuses to interfere in religious controversy.

DATE	LIFE OF MARTIN	POPE	EMPERORS	OTHER EVENTS
363			Jovian Augustus.	Sulpitius Severus born at Bordeaux. Julian dies 18th August.
364			Valentinian I Augustus. Valens Augustus.	February, death of Jovian. Ausonius summoned to court to teach Valentinian's son Gratian.
365		Death of Liberius and Felix.		
366		Damasus elected.		Election of pope Damasus after scenes of bloodshed.
368				Death of Hilary.
371	Martin elected to the bishopric of Tours 4th July.			
372	Martin visits Valentinian I.			
373				Death of Athanasius. Ambrose consecrated bishop of Milan and becomes religious adviser to Gratian.
375			Gratian succeeds as Augustus.	Valentinian dies suddenly in Pannonia.
378				Council meets at Rome to present a petition to Gratian for the imperial arms to be used to enforce ecclesiastical decisions. At Adrianople a Gothic army meet and defeat the Roman army under Valens who was killed.

379		Gratian Augustus. Theodosius Augustus.	Theodosius appointed by Gratian as Augustus at Sirmium.
380			Theodosius falls ill and is baptized. February, edict forbidding heresy and establishing two classes of Christians: catholics and heretics, and penalizing the latter. Priscillian denounced as a Manichee at the COUNCIL OF SARAGOSSA in Spain.
381			ECUMENICAL COUNCIL at CONSTANTINOPLE summoned by Theodosius. Arianism outlawed. Priscillian made bishop of Avila by his friends.
382	Jerome becomes secretary to pope Damasus.		Gratian orders removal of the statue of Victory. Debate of Symmachus.
383		Valentinian II Augustus. Maximus Augustus. Theodosius Augustus.	Maximus, the dux Brittaniorum is clothed with the purple by the troops in Britain, and enters Gaul. Gratian murdered at Lyons. Maximus enters Trèves.
384	Martin present at Council of Bordeaux but did not sign.	Siricius elected, hostile to ascetics.	COUNCIL OF BORDEAUX called by Maximus.
385	Martin at Trèves – lunches with Maximus and his wife.		COUNCIL AT TREVES, condemns Priscillian, who with his companions is executed. Birth of St Patrick in Britain.
386			Augustine, converted after reading the Life of St Antony, retires to Cassiacum.

DATE	LIFE OF MARTIN	POPE	EMPERORS	OTHER EVENTS
387				Maximus invades Italy and engages in battle with Valentinian II.
388				Capture and execution of Maximus by Theodosius. Valentinian II recognized as Augustus of the West.
389				Paulinus of Nola baptized by Delphinus of Bordeaux.
391				The senatorial party at Rome present petition to Valentinian II for restoration of the statue of Victory and the vestal virgins; resisted by Ambrose. Theodosius under the influence of Ambrose starts to issue strong edicts against the practice of paganism.
392			Eugenius Augustus. Theodosius Augustus.	Pagan revival in Rome. Jovinian leads movement against asceticism. Assassination of Valentinian II, place taken by usurper Eugenius, leader of pagan revival.
393				Conversion of Sulpitius Severus to asceticism. Paulinus of Nola and his wife take vow of continence.
394	Sulpitius visits Martin aged eighty-one.			Sulpitius Severus retires to Primulacium. Theodosius attacks Eugenius – battle of the River Frigidus. Final victory of catholic Christianity. Eugenius beheaded.

395	Martin dies at Candes, 11 November.	Siricius dies.	Honorius II, aged ten, Augustus. Arcadius, aged seventeen, Augustus.	*Confessions of St Augustine* written. (394–8) Sulpitius writing and publishing the *Life of St Martin*. January, Theodosius dies.
396				Vandal general Stilicho, guardian of Honorius, attacks Picts in Britain.
397				Ambrose dies at Milan.
399–407		Anastasius I elected.		Stilicho withdraws troops from Britain. The great invasion of Gaul. The usurper Flavius Claudius Constantine leads the remains of Roman army in Britain into Gaul.

Part One

Beginnings

I

On 31 December AD 406, the River Rhine froze over and across it at various points a vast horde of barbarians, Vandals, Alans and Suevi swarmed into Roman Gaul. They came regardless of loss of life. It was estimated that at least 20,000 of the Vandals alone lost their lives in the crossing, yet they still pressed on, forced by the relentless pressure of mouths to be fed and need for land. The great horde swept on right across Europe into Africa, leaving behind them a trail of devastation and confusion in what had been the civilized and fertile countryside of Roman Gaul. The only vestiges they left were the giant buildings, aqueducts and monuments, that they could not be bothered to destroy.

Almost at the same time, from farther south, another great migration of Germanic peoples was taking place in search of food, land and the wealth of the homelands of Italy. Alaric I, the Gothic chieftain, appeared with his army before the gates of Rome for the third time and, taking the city by surprise, entered by the Salarian gate on 24 August AD 410, and for three days his soldiers ransacked the city. It was a comparatively mild invasion and little harm was done to the buildings, but it left an indelible impression on the ancient world. Rome, the city whose august name had spelt security, peace, civilization and just laws in Europe, Britain, Africa and the Middle East, had at last an enemy within its walls – the first for 1,000 years. Everyone tried to reassure themselves that it was only a matter of time before the old ways would return, but they knew in their bones that this was the end of the ancient civilization of Greece and Rome – the Dark Ages had arrived and had come to stay.

In the two or three decades previous to these shattering events many sensitive and intelligent people had known that the end of the long years of stable government and cultural achievement was approaching. One unerring indication, which even the humblest slave could understand, was that inflation had been steadily mounting for a century or more and was now so out of control that many were beginning to return once more to the safer system of barter, and everyone knew that the wealthy were seeking every possible way of avoiding tax and the responsibilities and even dangers of public service. Time and again the ordinary soldiers, sensing through their pay packets that their leaders had lost control, themselves elected a new emperor, whose value they had proved in the field, feeling that, with soldierly efficiency and common sense he could take control of the empire and restore the situation. But things had gone too far; the trouble lay deeper than in mere bad management, it was a complex exhaustion of morale in the inner minds and spirits of men and women everywhere – for the civilization of Rome had run its course.

A pathetic and belated attempt to put the clock back came from the Roman army in Britain in 407. Hearing of the chaos on the other side of the Channel in Gaul, they elected one of their number as the new Augustus of the West. His name was Constantine, and to complete the illusion he renamed his two sons Constans and Julian, in memory of the triumphant march across Europe, starting from York, of the young emperor Constantine the Great a hundred years before. The quixotic band set out for Gaul and at first met with some success; it even looked for a time as if a real stay of execution had been achieved, but it was not to be. Constantine, sensing his failure, resigned from the throne, and with peculiar insight was ordained a presbyter, only to be murdered in cold blood with his young son Julian.

If there was any hope for the future of western civilization it was hard to see. It certainly did not lie in the hands of rulers and governors any more, rather it had come to rest in a group of men and women who had completely withdrawn from the civilized world and were quite careless whether it sank or swam.

On the south bank of the river Loire, at a place called Marmoutier, about three miles downstream from the city of Tours, there was a large grassy plain, which lay between the river and a line of forbidding grey cliffs that to this day rise sheer for a hundred feet or so, with trees clinging precariously to their face. The cliffs were honeycombed with caves, for all the world giving much the same appearance as the holes of sand-martin's nests in the side of a disused quarry. In the year AD 393 all the caves were inhabited and the grassy plain below was covered with the rough wooden shacks of a great camp of spiritual refugees, numbering in all some 2,000 men, whilst in the city of Tours itself was a similar, if smaller, group of women. The whole concourse was wrapped in a deep silence from morning until evening, punctuated only by the occasional singing of psalms or hymns, and the low voices of those who were reading the scriptures aloud; the atmosphere can best be described as that of an old-fashioned English village on a Sunday morning.

The reason for this great gathering of men, many of them young scions of the noble families of Gaul, lay not only in the general urge for withdrawal from public life among many of the higher classes at the time, but also in the attraction of the unconventional personality of Martin, the holy man and bishop of Tours. His quaint appearance at the age of seventy-seven belied the extraordinary depth and range of his character, for underneath the deliberately unkempt hair, the pallid features, and the rough serge slave's robe in which he was dressed, lay a personality that at one moment recalls the Mahatma Gandhi, at another, William Booth, at another, the visionary William Blake, and at yet another, Lord Montgomery of Alamein. In fact, so disguised was he by his humble garb and constant stillness and quiet that his own intimate followers sometimes mistook him. One of the younger members of the group on being asked to point him out said: 'If you are looking for that crazy fellow, just cast your eyes in that direction. In his usual half-witted way he is staring at the sky.'[1] It was an odd but understandable way to speak of one, who even then was acknowledged far and wide as the apostle of Gaul, for Martin's main preoccupation was always quiet contemplation, and even religious people often find the rationale of this occupation somewhat obscure.

Among the many young men who made the pilgrimage to the camp at Marmoutier were two friends, Paulinus and Sulpitius from Bordeaux some 350 kilometres away. They were both young men of noble families who had received the best possible classical education at Bordeaux university, made famous by the poet, author and royal tutor Ausonius. Their visits to Marmoutier, which did not take place at the same time, were to have far-reaching consequences, for they were both gifted speakers, trained in the art of rhetoric, and through their writings were to spread the message of Martin's life to a very wide audience, throughout the empire.

The first to arrive at Marmoutier was Paulinus, the elder of the two by ten years. Born in AD 353, he was the son of one of the highest ranking senators in the empire, the praetorian prefect in Gaul. As a young man he was himself appointed governor of the district of Campania in southern Italy, the district made famous by the poet Virgil's residence there when he was writing the *Georgics*, in praise of the idyllic country life; and clearly Paulinus fell in love with it. He went to Spain where he married Teresia, a young woman also of consular family, and not long after, they had their first child, a son. When the child died Paulinus and Teresia announced their 'conversion' to the ascetic ideal of Christianity; and they made a vow to abstain from any further sexual relationship whilst living in the same house as brother and sister; for they were going to try to imitate Christ to the letter. Paulinus sold many of his possessions, gave generously to the poor, and then retired to the family villa in the country near his beloved city of Nola in Campania. Here he and Teresia were joined by a few Christian friends of the same mind who lived a communal life with them in which Bible-reading, prayer and meditation formed a large part; they fasted till their faces had an unhealthy pallor, and ate only one meal a day, and their whole aim was to preserve in the church of their day the kind of straightforward and dedicated enthusiasm that had inspired so many ordinary Christians to offer themselves for martyrdom in the days of persecution. They converted part of the family villa into a church, which they dedicated in honour of the famous bishop of Nola, Felix, who during the persecutions had made a brave and public confession, and it was not altogether surprising when the people of Nola persuaded Paulinus to become their bishop. Paulinus could write of this kind of high living as of an idyllic existence: 'where I seemed to obtain rest from lying scandal and from wanderings, unbusied by public affairs and far from the din of the marketplace, I enjoyed the leisure of country life and my religious duties, surrounded by pleasant peace in my withdrawn household.'[2]

There is no doubt that his visit to Martin at Marmoutier somewhere around AD 386 had had a considerable part to play in the formation of Paulinus' setting up of his religious household, though it is known that there were other influences at work as well.[3] He was captivated by Martin and for the rest of his life spoke of him as 'my blessed father'; and the respect was certainly mutual, for Martin came to see Paulinus as the type of Christian to hold up as an example to all his followers of a dedicated Christian family man.

Whilst Paulinus and Teresia had been in the throes of their conversion experience, Sulpitius, ten years younger, had been clearly impressed by all that had happened to his friend, and the bubbling enthusiasm of Paulinus' letters. Having arrived at a watershed in his own life he decided to visit Martin himself. He was about thirty years of age with a promising career before him;[4] his success at the schools had been followed by the use of his rhetorical training in the law courts as a pleader, and according to Paulinus, because of his eloquence and mastery of language he had won wide acclaim. His writing bears this out, for Latinists have often pointed out its lucidity, and how he uses the classical style freely to express himself without artifice.[5] Beside all this he came from wealthy parents and was, like Paulinus, married to a young woman of consular family. Shortly after his marriage, however, his wife had died, and this seems to have been a powerful factor in his 'conversion'. He went to Tours hoping to catch a glimpse of the great man, sitting outside his hut on his three-legged stool in contemplation, or possibly to sit in with the crowd of his followers and visitors at one of his open dialogues on spiritual matters.

Perhaps because of his known friendship with Paulinus, however, Martin singled Sulpitius out and gave him a quite unexpected personal welcome, which completely overwhelmed him:[6]

> he cordially wished me joy, and rejoiced in the Lord that he had been held in such high estimation by me that I had undertaken a journey, owing to my desire of seeing him. . . .
> he went so far as in person to present me with water to wash my hands, and in the evening he himself washed my feet. . . .
> I felt so overcome by the authority he unconsciously exerted, that I thought it wrong to do anything but fall in with his plans.

After this memorable start Sulpitius paid a number of visits to Marmoutier during the next two years, and developed a quite uncritical admiration for his hero. As far as Martin had personal friends, Sulpitius could be numbered among them, and Martin would talk to him freely. Sulpitius listened to his dialogues with disciples and visitors, watched outside his cell when he was at prayer, got to know some of his closest followers and generally absorbed the atmosphere of Marmoutier and Tours into the pores of his skin. At the end of this period of three or four years, he emerged to announce his 'conversion', and set in train the arrangements for the winding up of his legal career; he retained only enough of his property to maintain himself and a few companions in poverty, with some left over to give to the poor and needy. Then, with his chosen companions, all Christians who had become themselves *conversi*, he left Bordeaux for Primulacium, his family's estate in the countryside between Toulouse and Narbonne. In the villa there they set up their commune like that of Paulinus at Nola, though composed it seems of entirely male company.

They were all ardent admirers of Martin and had dedicated themselves to live as much like him and his great commune at Marmoutier as possible, working out their own variations as they went along. To the casual passer-by, the villa lit up at night might look like any other prosperous country villa owned by a consular family, but inside all was different. Gone were the rich tapestries, the luxurious carpets and furnishings, and the lavish meals with all their courses, brought in by a procession of slaves. The household still retained a boy to wake them in the morning and wait at table, but they sat down in the empty rooms on their haunches on mats of sacking to eat their one modest dish of herbs, the day's only meal. The old formalities of nodding to the *lares* and *penates* had gone, as were the staid and decorous greetings between the members of the family; and, in their place, were readings of the scriptures, times of quiet for meditation and dialogue, and above all the kiss of peace, the Christians' greeting, which, in this household of stern sexual repression, took on a rapturous note. As at Nola, high on the list of priorities for discussion was the plan to convert a part of the villa buildings into a church, where Martin's name could be remembered by a picture on the wall of the baptistery, with verses written by Paulinus.[7]

Apart from the discovery of the delight of freedom from care to follow Christ in depth in the ordered round of devotions of his household, Sulpitius now found himself with time on his hands, and time for him meant talking, conversation, the practice of the art of rhetoric, an art which he had discovered was his chief talent. The practice of the art of rhetoric in such limited company meant only one thing, the writing of books, for one of the strangest features of Roman intellectual life in this era, which appears as an anachronism to modern eyes, is the fact that the art of shorthand was in widespread use. The great writers of the age were not so much writers as conversationalists, whose words were written down for public distribution; both Jerome and Augustine had shorthand writers in their entourage, which accounts for their prolific production, and Sulpitius himself had more than one to draw on.[8] It was inevitable that after he had settled in at Primulacium books written in this way, and springing out of the devotional life of the community, would start to appear.

Somewhere between his arrival at Primulacium and the death of Martin in AD 397, he produced his first book, *The Life of St Martin*. It consisted of a series of incidents he had gleaned either from Martin himself or his followers at Marmoutier, arranged in some sort of biographical framework, and was provided with a fulsome introduction and peroration. He sent a copy to Paulinus, who replied with his usual bubbling fervour: 'You have recounted, in language as apposite as your love is righteous, the history of the great priest, who is most clearly a confessor of the Church . . . he has merited an historian worthy of his faith and life.'[9] Paulinus took the book with him on one of his visits to Rome and there 'it was greedily laid hold of by the whole city; . . . I saw the booksellers rejoicing over it, for nothing was a source of greater profit to them, for nothing commanded a readier sale or fetched a higher price.'[10] From Rome it was carried all over the empire and greeted with enthusiasm in Carthage, Egypt and Memphis, and even an old man living alone on a deserted beach in North Africa had heard of it and asked for a copy; evidence seems to be appearing also that it arrived in Britain, and was much sought after.[11]

Sulpitius was overwhelmed at the book's reception. People started writing to him, mostly full of praise and asking for more, though in amongst the praise he detected a note of sharp criticism levelled by the more sceptical at some of the miracles which he had described Martin performing. Sulpitius began to answer them with letters, of which, unfortunately, only three survive, but in doing so a much more elaborate project was forming in his mind. He planned to write a dialogue, one of the most able ways of arguing a case or pursuing some line of enquiry known to classical writers. Plato had used it in his search for the ideal state, in the *Republic*, and Cicero had made full use of it in his historical and philosophical researches.

In preparation for this great work, Sulpitius sent one of the members of his commune at Primulacium, named Postumianus, on a tour of the Mediterranean seaboard, not only to study the reactions of the church at large to his first book, but also to make a careful investigation of the monastic life of the hermits which was developing in the Egyptian and Syrian deserts, so that he could make a proper evaluation of Martin's significance. Then, as soon as he heard Postumianus was on his way home, Sulpitius invited a number of people who had known Martin well to come to Primulacium for dialogue. The result of their discussions, worked on and arranged to form an artistic production, is to be found in the three *Dialogues of Sulpitius Severus*.[12] The three books give an even more detailed account of Martin's doings and throw a great deal of light on life in the contemporary church with a warmth and openness that was perhaps missing from the first work.

As an able advocate, Sulpitius is most careful to quote his witnesses by name and to assure sceptical readers that if they wish to they can interrogate them personally, but there is a mystery about the principal witness which is intriguing. This principal witness, the 'Gaul', acts as the narrator and tells most of the stories as an eye-witness, yet he remains anonymous throughout; 'our friend the Gaul'. It is as if he is to be approached, if required, either through Sulpitius or the others named, for he remains more than just an individual person, he has become the representative of that most important cultural group, soon to be submerged in the maelstrom of invasions, the Gallic or Celtic church.

Anyone setting about writing the life of Martin is bound to become involved sooner or later in trying to understand something of the richness of the culture of the Celtic peoples and particularly those of Gaul and Britain; for the life of Martin is the story of the Romano-Celtic peoples coming face to face with the individual heroism of the primitive Christian church, and ultimately warming to it in a mass conversion. Many books have recently been written about the Celts,[13] describing their warlike and quarrelsome habits, their love of individual combat and admiration of naked courage, their strange Druidic religion with its peculiar interest in the severed head, the dynamic role played by their womenfolk and the eerie beauty of their artefacts, which seem to sum up their sense of the all-pervading mystery of the other world; and it seems many more will be written as new facts come constantly to light. Sulpitius, when he was writing, was fully conscious of the cultural background of the people whom he was mainly addressing, for he was writing for the church in Gaul.

The church had been slow to grow in Romano-Celtic Gaul, but as it did so it developed marked characteristics of its own. At first consisting of small groups gathered under their bishops in the Roman towns, it had had its share of heroic encounters in the persecutions. It emerged into the fourth century with an ardent loyalty to both the emperor and the bishop of Rome, but with a strong desire to remain independent of them both in its judgments. Well-led throughout the religious

2 *The chi-rho monogram, secret symbol of the early Christian church, placed by Constantine on the standards of the army. It was used by the Christians of the fourth century to identify with the primitive church and its 'unbroken perfection'*

controversies of the fourth century, it seemed on the whole to steer a course that maintained the enthusiasm and loyalty of the church of the catacombs, and indeed at one time some of its leaders were to be subjected to persecution for their uncompromising stand. It is with real Celtic disdain for the worldliness and toadying of the court bishops, who relied heavily for their position on the imperial purse strings that Sulpitius wrote of the idea of their claiming subsistence allowances from the Government: 'it seemed unseemly to the men of our part of the world, that is the Aquitanians, the Gauls and the Britons, so that refusing the public supplies, they preferred to live at their own expense', when summoned by the emperor to a council.[14] So it was well to keep the Gaul's identity hidden, for though he might be approached like the others in a roundabout way, he remained a mystery figure with whom every Gallic reader could identify as expressing the warmth and ardour of a quite new cultural force within the church.

After the *Dialogues*, Sulpitius settled down to compose his *Sacred History*, a 'condensed account of those things which are set forth in the Sacred Scriptures from the beginning of the world . . . down to a period within our own remembrance.'[15] Apart from the asides it is a dull but useful compendium, which became a textbook for the schools of the Middle Ages, but in the last chapters, when he comes to tell of the triumphs of the Gallican church in its fight with heresy and worldliness, Sulpitius' whole narrative takes on the warmth and vividness of experienced history, especially when his hero, Martin, appears on the scene once more. Sulpitius died, so men say, about the year AD 425.

Sulpitius' books and letters reflect his own naïve and sincere personality, but show that, as befitted a lawyer, for all his high-flown language he was prudent in the way he presented his case. They shed a clear and steady light on Martin's character, and show how in an age of great names his was an outstanding personality; and in doing this, they almost by accident provide an unique account of day to day life in a parish in the primitive church.

2

Martin, then, was born at Sabaria in Pannonia, but was brought up at Ticinum, which is situated in Italy. His parents were, according to the judgement of the world, of no mean rank, but were heathens. His father was at first simply a soldier, but afterwards a military tribune.[1]

So Sulpitius begins the *Life of St Martin*, and though he is studiously vague about dates, important evidence seems to suggest that Martin was born in the year AD 316.[2] Sabaria, the modern Stein-am-Anger, was an important frontier garrison town, founded by the Romans, the capital at that time of the province of Pannonia and a frequent residence of the emperors. There were always heavy concentrations of troops there to man the castles along the western bank of the Danube, which formed the empire's frontier.

The legions of Pannonia were a famous training ground for the elite corps of officers, and from their ranks a number of emperors had emerged, some of whom had risen from humble peasant origin. The emperor Decius had been born there of an Italian family, and the emperors Claudius II, Gothicus, Aurelian, Probus, Diocletian and Constantine, all of Illyrian peasant stock, were men of exceptional force and talent, who staved off the collapse of imperial defence against all probabilities.[3] Martin's father was a member of this elite corps; starting from the ranks, he had risen to be a military tribune, which, short of supreme command, was as high as anyone could normally aspire without an aristocratic background. He and his wife were determined pagans and could be expected to have resented bitterly the failure of the persecutions to put an end to Christianity, a form of religion which many good traditional Romans saw as the most dangerous threat to the old imperial order; they even named their son Martin, after Mars the Roman god of farm and battleground, in the hope, no doubt, that he would grow up to champion the old cause.

The whole fabric of the empire, which stretched from northern Britain to Spain, from North Africa to the Middle East, the southern banks of the Danube and the Rhine, had been created by and rested at this time upon two factors only, the personality of the reigning emperor, and the loyalty and strength of the army. Only three years before Martin's birth one of the most famous of all the Roman emperors Diocletian, had died; famous for his determination to restore the fortunes of the empire by his organizing ability and reforms, and infamous among the Christian people as the most ruthless of all those who had persecuted them with the set purpose of their total destruction. In both these attempts he had failed and had spent the declining years of his life in a sad retirement, nursing his sense of frustration and disappointment.

Diocletian had certainly been faced with a great problem in how to manage his vast and straggling empire. The problem of communication alone would appear, on the face of it, to have been quite insuperable. Even with modern, highly sophisticated communication systems, it is almost impossible for central government departments to keep in touch with what is actually going on in the districts among the rank and file of ordinary people; it seems miraculous that the Romans were able to manage at all. Yet they had their magnificent road system, with its relays of horses at intervals of six to sixteen miles, with an inn or *mansio* for an overnight stop every twenty or thirty miles.

These roads led from one military camp or town to another, and from thence on to the garrisons on the borders, and it was through the army that the messages of the central administration arrived and from whom the reactions to them were received; so that everything depended upon maintaining the goodwill of the army, and making sure that the individual soldiers were paid, housed and fed.

Diocletian's reaction, therefore, on his election had been to set about the reform of the army. It is estimated that he raised its size from between 300,000–400,000 to 500,000 men or more, creating a field force that was prepared to march anywhere to the seats of trouble; he drew from the barbarian allies the beginnings of cavalry regiments, creating citizen armies from the tribes that lived close to the borders, and created a personal bodyguard for himself from among the best fighters in the world – the Germans. This vast army needed feeding and clothing, housing and payment, and the history of the fourth century, the period covered by Martin's life, the period of the decline and fall of the empire, was the history of frantic efforts by successive emperors to raise enough money through taxation to pay their soldiers.

To raise the necessary funds, Diocletian started the first known annual budgets in history,[4] and combined them with the most crushing taxation. In order to ensure that the taxes were collected he needed a large-scale expansion of the civil service.

For some unaccountable reason, which is not even understood today, Diocletian's reforms were undertaken against a background of severe inflation. It was something which was world-wide and apparently quite incapable of being halted, as the history of soldiers' pay shows. Diocletian tried to check it in two ways, by devaluing the currency and fixing prices through his famous edict of AD 301. Detailed maximum prices were fixed for items ranging from pork sausages to cloaks, the wage limits were fixed for all classes of employees from the ordinary labourer to the professional advocate, and to drive the message home the penalty for infringement was to be death or deportation. Needless to say, his action had not the slightest impact.

Another of Diocletian's projects for the strengthening of his empire had been his division of it into four separate areas of government, each with its own Caesar, a pattern of devolution which was to be repeated off and on for the whole of the century, and in theory it was a most sensible arrangement. He himself remained as over-all Augustus and resided at Nicomedia, near what was to become Constantinople, in the east; Maximian, an Illyrian peasant, he raised to be his co-Augustus in the west, living at Milan; Constantius Chlorus (father of Constantine the Great) was created Caesar in the west, with his headquarters at Trier, and Galerius in the east, with his headquarters at Sirmium. Each of these Caesars had a standing field army with him, which he commanded, and thus, what was intended to be a means of easing the administrative problems of the empire, became the means of its undoing, as various rival emperors were elected from the armies of the different districts. There is little doubt, however, that Diocletian's real intention was to focus all attention upon himself as supreme ruler, and he surrounded himself with such a panoply of kingship as had never been seen before, setting up imperial courts with buildings that would be a sign for everyone of the prestige of his personality.

To give to the peoples of this vast and scattered empire some spiritual cohesion, some emotional centre upon which the sentiments of the very different racial groups could converge, Diocletian had set himself the task of the establishment of a revived pagan worship, which was to be acceptable for all his subjects to include in the rituals of their local pantheons. The universal gods he promoted had the genial title, *Genius popvli Romani*, the title borne by the widespread and universal coinage, the debased nature of which was itself a symptom perhaps of a lack of real confidence.

In issuing this coinage with such a religious emblem Diocletian knew perfectly well that he was heading for a confrontation with that organization that had been slowly but surely spreading throughout his empire, and with whom he knew at some time there had to be a reckoning, the Christian church. All the things which were wrong with the empire were right with the church, and this very rightness, which had a ring of truth and profundity about it, commended itself to people of all ranks and walks of life and cultures within the empire. The empire was kept in being by the often cruel and impersonal rule of a dictator, enforced by an obedient and impersonal army; the Christian church was kept in being by the voluntary support of its members, upon whom there was no physical coercion to join. The church leaders, the bishops and other officials, exercised for the most part a ministry of encouragement and support, and were approachable and unaffected men, often persecuted and imprisoned for doing their work. The only contact many people had with the emperor was through the payment of harsh and crippling taxes enforced by often unscrupulous men. The offerings of Christians were gladly given according to the means and spirit of the giver. The unity of the empire was reasonably apparent, but was a superficial and brittle creation, with no deep significance, and was often maintained by means of secret police and informers; the unity of the church was something that, in spite of internal disagreements, went deep and provided its members with a sense of belonging to a world-wide institution with ever-spreading frontiers far beyond the bounds of the empire. Above all, in spite of the efforts of various high-minded political and spiritual leaders, it was clear that behind the empire's fine and courageous façade, lay no satisfying philosophy for everyday living and no real guidelines for ordinary people to mould their lives on. Christianity, on the other hand, provided not only an explanation of life, and a satisfying philosophy, but also the supporting role of a way of worship of God, and an educational system based on scriptures that made demands on people's intelligence and emotions.

As the church grew in numbers and in influence alongside and within the empire, it menaced those who were responsible for the administration and for retaining the obedience and loyalty of its peoples. One of the fears of every pagan emperor was that too many of his soldiers might become involved in the life of the church; and so it was that Diocletian took the drastic step of a head-on confrontation with the church, intending, with his colleagues, to stamp it out altogether. After much hesitation and consulting of the gods, some nineteen years after his accession, when he felt well-established, he had started to issue the edicts that inaugurated the great persecution. All assemblies of Christians were forbidden, churches were to be destroyed, and sacred books burnt, known followers were to be dismissed from state employment, including above all those in the army, priests were to be arrested in the eastern province and forced to sacrifice to the gods of the state, and finally in AD 304 this order was extended to every member of the Christian faith.[5]

The persecution ceased in AD 311 for the most part, exhausted with the blood-letting of an obviously innocent group of people. Of all the countless incidents that went to make up one of the major turning points in the history of civilization, perhaps one incident may suffice to point out the bitterness of the struggle; it took place in Cappadocia when Martin was four years old, some time after the main persecution had ceased. The soldiers in all the legions as a matter of course were instructed to sacrifice to the gods of the empire; but forty, all from different districts refused.[6] Brought before the governor, they were shown the imperial edict and invited again to subscribe; they all as one man stated firmly, 'We are Christians', and refused. The governor then offered them bribes to which they replied: 'All that you offer us is of a world that is perishing, we despise that world. We only look for a reward in heaven, and we only fear hell.' It was a bitter winter and their punishment was to be stripped and marched on to the ice of a neighbouring lake, where they were to be left exposed for the night. Beside them a sentry was placed with a glowing fire and a warm bath. They chanted their prayer through the night: 'Forty martyrs went out to fight; may forty martyrs wear the crown.' One of their number under the agony of cold succumbed and went and warmed himself, but they continued their prayer, and the pagan sentry, his heart moved by what he saw, stripped off his cloak and ran down on to the ice to replace him. In the morning their dead bodies were collected to be burnt, and the mother of one of the youngest, watching them being placed on the cart and seeing a flicker of life in her son, rushed forward to help place him on the pile.

Such vivid war stories as these formed the background of Martin's childhood. As each new act of oafish stupidity of the Christians was pointed out by his father, his imagination became more and more inflamed, not only out of pity, but also because children sometimes have a directness of vision of the difference between complete integrity and the blustering affirmations of believers in half-worked-out creeds. Martin longed to know more of who these Christians were, and if possible to meet one, for even at his tender age, the thought of being a soldier-martyr sounded far more exciting than the dull routine of life of those soldiers who spent so much time marching up and down his father's parade ground.

Martin was to be denied the opportunity of becoming a soldier-martyr for, to all intents and purposes, by the year AD 325 when he was nine years old the persecutions were finally over. Diocletian had retired to his personal garrison fortress at Salona, where he shut himself away and died, a broken and disillusioned man. All the talk was now of a new age that had dawned, as if by the miraculous intervention of the God of the Christians. The story went about that the Christian God had raised up an emperor in Britain, the young man Constantine, eighteen years of age, who had marched on Rome at the head of his victorious legions, had seen a great cross in the sky and heard the Divine voice saying 'In this sign conquer', and had gone on to conquer all his enemies and to become sole Augustus. He had then not only stopped the persecutions of Christians, but had gone out of his way to restore their churches to them, and wonder of wonders, it seemed as if he so favoured them as if he wanted to make everyone in the empire embrace the faith of their church. For many it was too much to take in, as for Martin's father, especially when Constantine went on to assemble 300 of the leading bishops of the church at Nicaea, not far from the imperial palace of Nicomedia, presided himself over their discussions and lavished upon them gifts from the imperial bounty.

But for Martin, fascinated by the Christians' victory without arms, to be nine years old at this time was heaven. Now that Christianity had become respectable, his parents could hardly refuse him the right to wander off and explore the church in the town for himself, especially when the chi-rho, the secret Christian symbol, was now sprawled over the sacred standards laid up in the regimental shrine of his father's legion.

By now too the family had been living for some years in the town of Ticinum, the modern Pavia, in northern Italy. It was an important little garrison town, twenty-five miles away from Milan on the great Roman road that ran from Rome to Milan and then on to Gaul, in one direction, or to Padua and thence to Pannonia in the other. Perched on a hill it boasted a triumphal arch in honour of Augustus and a stone bridge across the river Ticinum below, but above all it had a church. Not that the casual passer-by would have recognized it as such, except to wonder at the people continually coming and going from it; for what are often referred to as churches in the first three centuries were almost without exception no more than large villas converted into meeting places. To the passer-by they would have appeared no different to any other grand town villa, but inside, the difference would have been striking.

Some of the rooms would be reserved as the residence of the bishop; others, called *secretaria*, would be reserved as the offices where the deacons could conduct church business or meet to have consultations with members of the congregation. The entrance hall with its usual fountain of running water – now often marked with the chi-rho monogram – would have been converted into what was considered one of the most important rooms in the house, the baptistery, where baptisms were conducted. In the heart of the building was the most important room of all, the place where the Eucharist or breaking of bread took place. This was divided up into two or more quite separate compartments. The porch or vestibule was reserved for uncommitted strangers who were free to come in to watch and listen to what went on during the readings and explanations; in this place too stood the catechumens, those who had enrolled for special instruction for baptism, and the *energoumenoi*, the mentally and physically handicapped. The large inner room was reserved as the place of worship for those who had received baptism, and at its far end it had a simple table surrounded with chairs for the bishop, his presbyters and deacons.

When Martin as a child of ten first entered the building and was shown where he was to stand in the vestibule of the church, his first sight of the Christian assembly must have fired his already awakened imagination, for he would find himself packed in among an extraordinarily assorted crowd. The strangers and catechumens were together, men and women of all ages and a number of children; rich man, poor man, beggar man, mixed up in a way that could be seen nowhere else in Roman society. On the other side were the *energoumenoi*, the mentally sick, some sitting dumbly, others grimacing, others shouting so that they had to be removed, a sight that likewise was to be seen nowhere else. At first it must have alarmed him, but as he watched the men called the exorcists working among them, he must have been deeply impressed for in later life it was the one role in the church that he was prepared to undertake of his own free will, and his skill in the treatment of the mentally disturbed betrays a special vocation experienced when young, during his long catechumenate.

Through a large open doorway, they could all see into the inner church, filled with the faithful baptized members of the congregation. The room was a blaze of candlelight in memory of the Eucharists of scripture and of those services held at night in private houses during the persecutions, and indeed there were some standing there who had suffered at that time. Martin watched as the bishop passed, who had been the church's pastor since the persecution days; his name was Anastasius,[7] and with him went his presbyters and deacons, all dressed in the flowing robes of Roman gentlemen, to take their places round the holy table.

The service began with songs, prayers and scripture-readings read by the clerics or members of the congregation, and answered to by all in the church, until at last the bishop gave his instruction. Apart from the stories of the Old Testament and of Christ and his apostles, all entirely new to him, Martin would hear him tell of the sufferings of martyrs and their triumphs, and every now and again a quite new note would creep in as the bishop told of one or another who, denied the privilege of martyrdom had given up everything and gone out into the deserts of Egypt or Syria to live a life of voluntary martyrdom, in abject poverty and complete solitude; eremites – hermits they were called – men who lived in the deserts.

When the bishop had finished speaking he came and blessed those who were packed in the vestibule and one of the deacons then bade them all to leave. As they left each Sunday, Martin watched the doors closing on that crowd in the warmly lit inner room, who were about to celebrate the mysteries; his mind set on two things: he wanted to be baptized so as to be able to join in with them, and he wanted to be a man of the desert, as Sulpitius wrote:[8]

> when he was of the age of ten years, he betook himself, against the wish of his parents, to the Church, and begged that he might become a catechumen. Soon afterwards, becoming in a wonderful manner completely devoted to the service of God, when he was twelve years old, he desired to enter on the life of a hermit; and he would have followed up that desire with the necessary vows, had not his as yet too youthful age prevented.

Baptism or initiation as a member of the Christian church was for the first four centuries a ceremony of absolutely central importance in the life both of the individual convert and of the local church which he or she was joining. There was a sense of 'either–or' finality about it, which had been heightened by the centuries of persecution, and such intensity of feeling had raised all sorts of pastoral problems which were to present grave problems for the church throughout the fourth century. At this period, however, baptism was still regarded everywhere with the utmost awe. It was a ceremony held usually only once a year at the festival of the resurrection, the Christian Passover, Easter Day, and must actually be performed by the bishop himself, or if the numbers were too many, presided over by him in person. So strong was the sense of complete forgiveness and total commitment implied in the sacrament that many people delayed it indefinitely, living their lives on the fringe of the church's worship as catechumens until death approached. Many indeed held it in such awe that they felt they should accompany it with vows of sexual abstinence, fastings and prayers.

Whilst the baptism of infants in the face of imminent death was developing, the main attitude of this immediate post-persecution church was still that of Tertullian:[9] 'in the case of children shall one to whom earthly substance is not entrusted be entrusted with heavenly?

Let them know how to seek salvation, that you may be seen to "give to him that asketh".'

The period of preparation for baptism was long and arduous, especially for a child like Martin, unaccompanied by his parents. On his requesting it, his name would be taken and placed on the church roll by one of the deacons. He would be questioned as to his motives, and as to the status of his parents. He would then before the whole assembly of Christians on Sunday be enrolled along with any others by the bishop, who made the sign of the cross on the forehead and laid hands on him with prayer. From that moment he was officially a catechumen, or one preparing for baptism, in the order of the hearers or *audientes*. For the period of two years at least his attendance and devotion would be watched over by one of the members of the congregation appointed as a teacher or catechist, and at the end of it if he felt ready as Martin did, he was free to offer himself for baptism.

If he was accepted he would then be enrolled among the catechumens called *competentes*, who were allowed to stay to join in the mysteries, and were given a course of special instruction by the bishop during what is now known as Lent, in readiness for their baptism.[10] Martin duly presented himself to the deacon or bishop and explained his twofold objective, and his enthusiasm was tested by having his eager request turned down. It did not change his purpose one whit and he was content to continue as a catechumen probably learning each week in the church porch from the exorcists how to handle the pathetic members of the congregation whose plight would always move him to acts of compassion.

All the time, however, his mind was 'always engaged in matters pertaining to the monasteries of the Church, already meditating in his boyish years what he afterwards, as a professed servant of Christ, fulfilled'.[11] Sulpitius, with his pious hindsight, is probably elaborating what Martin told him, that he had always longed to be a hermit, and there is certainly nothing unusual about this in one so young at this time. Some children, especially those with a vivid visual imagination, love to be alone with invisible companions, and would, given the chance, like Benedict two hundred years later, run off and hide in a well, especially if their minds had been fired by the much praised heroic solitudes of others.

Martin arrived at his fifteenth birthday a withdrawn adolescent with a rich imaginative life, but with a distaste for soldiering that greatly incensed his father. He was drawing near to the end of his schooling, and in a year or so would be ready on 17 March to don the all-white man's toga and be introduced to all his father's companions as having 'come of age'. No doubt he was waiting for just this moment to come home and remove the toga, place on himself the robe of a slave and make for the desert, but the emperor Constantine, the Christian hero and protector of the church, in conjunction with his own father, had other things in store for him.

3

In the year AD 326 the emperor Constantine, flushed with the success of his council of bishops at Nicaea was faced with the harsh realities of barbarian forces massing on the frontiers. As a consequence, notices began to appear, posted up in every garrison town and signed by himself and his son Constantius, demanding that the sons 'of veteran soldiers, when the notice of conscription goes up on the board in all the cities, must be constrained by force . . . to assume the functions of the decurionate or to serve in the army.'[1] The age of enrolment was fixed to include everyone between the ages of twenty and twenty-five. Time-honoured attempts were made to evade the call-up, ranging from flight to serious self-wounding, and the notices clearly did not produce their desired effect. Five years later, the Danube frontier was at serious risk and it was no surprise when a further edict appeared, bringing the age down to sixteen.

Reading these notices, one senior tribune, serving out his last posting in Ticinum, had at last found a means whereby his national pride and his personal frustration at his son's unmanly posturing could be satisfied at one stroke. Martin's father laid information about him to the recruiting officer, who arrived, having been warned in advance of his stubborn nature, complete with a set of manacles [2] To Martin's surprise his leave-taking from home was not the long-planned flight into the freedom and adventure of the desert, but being bundled unceremoniously into a military waggon, and driven off for twenty-five years' harsh compulsory service. His parents no doubt felt as many parents have felt before and since, that army service would quickly make a man of him, and in a sense they were right.

Every man is the prisoner for life of the institutions of his childhood and youth, and, however much he reacts against them, the mark they leave remains indelible on his character. Being brought up in the background of Roman garrison life would have left its mark on Martin anyway; but to be thrown unceremoniously in the emotional upheaval of adolescence into the army's rough and tumble ensured that he would be challenged at every turn by the outlook and culture of one of the most powerful civilizing institutions the world has yet known.

The Roman army at this stage in its history was a massive organization, comprising some 500,000 men, largely engaged in the maintenance of frontier garrisons, but also involved from time to time in bloody civil wars. The main army was divided into legions, each consisting 'of a nominal strength of 5,000 men, divided into ten cohorts of six centuries (80–100 men). A legion had its own force of specialists – armourers, blacksmiths, medical orderlies etc. – and included a small troop of cavalry used for scouting.'[3] Its tradition had been built upon the original farmer-soldiers of the republic, but as time went on many of its troops, and indeed commanders, had been recruited from among its subjugated peoples.

Its success as a civilizing influence consisted in the fact that its soldiers did not confine their interest simply to fighting. The uniform layout of their camps, especially when they stayed long in one place, naturally formed the ground plan of many a Roman town or city. Their farming ability made them able colonists, and they shared their skill with their conquered peoples, who came to admire them greatly and copy them. When not engaged in fighting they built roads, established and maintained the highly complex posting and signalling system, built bridges and aqueducts, baths and hospitals, dug canals, created sewage systems, and everywhere they went in town or country they built shrines for their gods, in which they were only too glad to accommodate the gods or *genii* of the local towns and villages.

From the ancient world there comes no better eye-witness account of the impact the legions made on the people they conquered than that given by the Jewish historian Josephus. It describes well the kind of institution into which Martin was now pitchforked:[4]

> If anyone does but attend to the other parts of their military discipline, he will be forced to confess that their obtaining so large a dominion, hath been the acquisition of their labour, and not the bare gift of fortune; for they do not begin to use their weapons first in time of war. . . . but as if their weapons did always cling to them, they have never any truce from warlike exercises; nor do they stay till times of war admonish them to use them; for their military exercises differ not at all from the real use of their arms, but every soldier is every day exercised, and that with great diligence, as if it were in time of war, which is the reason why they bear the fatigue of battle so easily; for neither can any disorder remove them from their usual regularity, nor

can fear affright them out of it, nor can labour tire them. . . . Nor can their enemies easily surprise them with the suddenness of their incursions; for as soon as they have marched into an enemy's land, they do not begin to fight till they have walled their camp about; nor is the fence they raise rashly made, or uneven; nor do they all abide in it, nor do those that are in it take their places at random; but if it happens that the ground is uneven, it is first levelled; their camp is also four square by measure, and carpenters are ready, in great numbers, with their tools to erect their buildings for them.

3 When they have secured themselves, they live together by companies with quietness and decency, as are all their other affairs managed with good order and security. Each company hath also their wood, and their corn and their water brought to them, when they stand in need of them; for they neither sup or dine as they please themselves singly, but all together. Their times also for sleeping, and watching, and rising, are notified before hand by the sound of trumpets, nor is anything done without a signal; and in the morning the soldiery go everyone to their centurions, and these centurions to their tribunes, to salute them; with whom all the superior officers go to the general of the whole army, who then gives them of course the watchword and other orders, to be by them carried to all that are under their command. . . .

4 When they are to go out of their camp, the trumpet gives a sound, at which nobody lies still, but at the first intimation they take down their tents, and all is made ready for their going out; then do the trumpets sound again, to order them to get ready for the march; then do they lay their baggage suddenly upon their mules and other beasts of burden, and stand, at the place for starting, ready to march; when also they set fire to the camp. . . . Then do the trumpets give a sound the third time, that they are to go out in order to excite those that on any account are a little tardy, that so no one may be out of his rank when the army marches. Then does the crier stand at the general's right hand, and asks them thrice in their own tongue whether they be ready to go out to war or not. To which they reply as often, with a loud and cheerful voice saying 'We are ready'. And this they do almost before the question is asked them; they do this as filled with a kind of martial fury and at the same time that they so cry out, they lift up their right hands also.

When the manacles were removed, Martin would have in his hands the letter of introduction handed by his father to the recruiting officer, and this would ensure his preferential treatment.[5] For the first years of his service he would be drilled, marched about and exercised with all the rest, until he had finished his initial training. At the passing-out parade came the first of the *sacramenta*, or oaths made before the legion in the presence of the sacred standards. A selected man would read out the oath to the emperor's person, to which all would reply, *'idem in me'* (I also); and it was made quite clear to them 'that the law has given their commanders the power to put to death without trial those who disobey or desert the colours'. Other *sacramenta* followed, especially when he joined his legion, clutching after the journey what was left of his *viaticum*, or journey money, of three gold pieces.

3 *Martin when he left the army (drawn from a detail in the mural by Simone Memmi (1284–1344) in the lower church at Assisi. The hair is coloured ochre)*

As a tribune's son he had many privileges: the right to serve in his father's corps, with immediate promotion to the rank of *circuitor* or under-officer; the right to receive a double ration of food, and to bring a servant with him, and his own horse or horses.[6] They all helped to provide him with leisure to carry out his chosen vocation and to prepare himself for baptism; and[7]

> This he did, by helping those who were in trouble, by furnishing assistance to the wretched, by supporting the needy, by clothing the naked, while he reserved nothing for himself from his military pay except what was necessary for his daily sustenance . . . far from being a senseless 'hearer' of the gospel, he so far complied with its precepts as to take no thought for the morrow.

The beggars and *energoumenoi* that hung about the church in Amiens where he was stationed had found a friend.

Martin, determined not to be rejected when he applied for baptism, this time on the grounds of his being a rough soldier, had started already to live the life of the 'converted'; he had even drawn his batman-slave in to live it with him as in a brotherhood, for it is odd how, in spite of his constant hankering after the hermit's life, he always seemed to end up with a man Friday. His fellow officers liked him for his genial nature, but when they noticed the quizzical way he used to take turns in cleaning his batman's boots and waiting on him at table, they said he was not so much a soldier as a monk.

What happened then is part of the world's folk history,[8]

At a certain period when Martin had nothing except his arms and his simple military dress, in the middle of the winter, a winter which had shown itself more severe than ordinary, so that the extreme cold was proving fatal to many, Martin happened to meet at the gate of the city of Amiens a poor man destitute of clothing. He was entreating those that passed by to have compassion on him, but all passed the wretched man without notice, when Martin, that man full of God, recognized that a being to whom others showed no pity, was, in that respect, left to him.

4 *The oldest known representation of the 'Charity of St Martin'. Miniature of the sacramentary of Fulda c. 975. Martin is on foot, in accordance with the account in the* Life of St Martin *by Sulpitius Severus*

Yet what should he do? He had nothing except the cloak in which he was clad for he had already parted with the rest of his garments for similar purposes. Taking, therefore, his sword with which he was girt, he divided his cloak into two equal parts, and gave one part to the poor man, while he again clothed himself with the remainder. Upon this, some of the bystanders laughed, because he was now such an unsightly object, and stood out as but partly dressed. Many, however, who were of sounder mind groaned deeply because they themselves had done nothing similar.

They especially felt this, because being possessed of more than Martin, they could have clothed the poor man, without reducing themselves to nakedness. In the following night, when Martin had resigned himself to sleep, he had a vision of Christ arrayed in that part of his cloak with which he had clothed the poor man. He contemplated his Lord with the greatest attention, and was told to own as his, the robe which he had given. Ere long, he heard Jesus saying with a clear voice to the multitude of angels standing round: 'Martin, who is still but a catechumen clothed me with this robe.'

Dreams were to many in the ancient world a drawing aside of the veils of reality, and for Martin the 'still but a catechumen' and the visible presence of Christ Himself constituted his complete 'conversion', a conversion which meant literally taking the plunge into that which he had so long planned and worked for, the waters of baptism. With absolute confidence he approached the bishop of Amiens, who had watched him as a catechumen in the hearer class, and he was accepted for the final preparation.

The baptism service was the climax of six weeks or so of intense preparation of the selected catechumens, in which the whole local church community was involved, and it took place at the Christian Passover, Easter day. As the candidates during these six weeks were involved in special examination, prayer, fasting and instruction by the bishop, so the congregation became implicated in what amounted to an examination of their own baptismal vows, and it is more than likely that this period of preparation quickly became the traditional forty days' fast of Lent.

At the beginning of Lent on one of the Sundays, the candidates appeared in front of the bishop and the whole congregation for the first of the 'scrutinies'. The deacon brought out the church register and as each applicant came before him interrogated him as to his name and occupation, and desire. Any member of the congregation was free to raise objections, but if none were raised the candidates were exorcized by being blessed with the laying on of hands of the presbyters and the signing of the cross. From this time onwards they were, as a group, in the forefront of the church's life and were admitted to stay and watch during the celebration of the mysteries.[9] Further 'scrutinies' took place on the Sundays following, and after the service the bishop took the candidates into the baptistery, and, as they stood around the fountain, gave them instruction in the faith from the scriptures. They were left in no uncertainty not only of the personal interest taken in them and their future by the local church, but also, as the great day approached, sensed something of the trust being reposed in them, when they were given the creed and the Lord's prayer, and had the faith explained in confidence.

Late on Easter eve they assembled in the baptistery, and after the readings in the church, the bishop and clergy came to the fountain and blessed the living water. The candidates in their separate places, the children first, then the men and then the women undressed themselves completely and standing naked, abjured Satan saying 'I renounce thee, Satan', each one in turn, and then walked down the two or three steps into the pool, where the fountain poured, until the water was above the waist. One of the presbyters then asked each candidate:

'Dost thou believe in God the Father almighty?

Dost thou believe in Jesus Christ, his only Son
our Lord, who was born and suffered?

Dost thou believe in the Holy Spirit, the holy
Church, the forgiveness of sins, the resurrection
of the flesh?'

And to each reply in the affirmative, he or she was placed under the water or had it splashed over their heads. Dripping and naked they came up out of the water, were immediately anointed with oil by the bishop, as a sign of the seal of the Spirit, and then, dressed in a clean white robe (*candidatus*), they joined the rest of the congregation in the brightly lit church. There they experienced the joyful fulfilment of years of preparation, as they received the kiss from the brethren and partook of the sacred bread and wine.

After his baptism Martin did not

all at once retire from military service, yielding to the entreaties of his tribune, whom he considered as his familiar tent companion. For the tribune promised that, after the period of his office had expired, he too would retire from the world. Martin, kept back by the expectation of this event,

continued, although but in name to act the part of a soldier
for nearly two years after he had received baptism.

What exactly Sulpitius meant by those two years has been cause of
many conjectures, for it seems quite clear that Martin remained at
any rate connected with the army for the full term of service – some
twenty-five years.

A clue lies in the extraordinary statement that this young officer
shared his tent with his tribune or commander, in the hopes of winning
his conversion. The only official in the Roman army who would be
expected to do this would be the tribune's personal *medicus* or doctor.
The army *medicus* with his team of assistant legionaries was a very
important person. Some of the most advanced knowledge of medicine
and surgery was possessed by these men who had more than anyone
the opportunity and facilities to practise their art, often in the field of

5   *Two medical officers at work
at a field dressing station (drawn
from a detail on Trajan's
column)*

battle.[10] Martin's already developed interest in the poor, the sick and
the mentally deranged, and the outstanding sanity of his diagnostic
skill which made his later healings smack of the miraculous, presuppose
some form of medical training. It seems reasonable to suppose that
his equable temperament and sensitivity to suffering convinced his
brother officers, who held him in high regard, that after his baptism
he might stay with the legion and remain on its books not only as the
tribune's personal *medicus*, but to help generally in this kind of work
amongst the soldiers and, where there was special need, among
civilians.

During his time of military service as an increasingly committed
member of the Christian church, Martin could not help but come
to appreciate the liberating value of its, at first sight irksome, discipline,
and to begin to work out its implications for the practice of his
Christian life. St Paul had noted the connection long before: 'In the
army,' he wrote,[11] 'no soldier gets himself mixed up in civilian life,
because he must be at the disposal of the man who enlisted him';

and elsewhere in the empire just at this time, another disbanded conscript, Pachomius, converted during his army service to Christianity, was putting his knowledge of army discipline to good account in the deserts of Egypt, where he was gathering groups of hermits into ordered communities.[12]

The whole institution of the Roman army was built on three basic principles, all designed to keep the soldier free for his work. The moment his chains were removed, Martin knew from the first cut of the centurions wand to the threats of the *sacramenta,* that the army stood and fell on obedience, complete and final. The long drills, exercises and punishments were designed simply to drive this one lesson home, and to break the soldier's will until he responded automatically. The odd thing was, as many have noticed, that obedience brought its own rewards of inner freedom. The Roman soldier was a poor man at least until his retirement. His food was mainly wheat, with meat as a very rare luxury, and he must eat and sleep with others. Yet again poverty had its rewards, for the Roman soldier was perhaps the best looked after citizen in the ancient world. Then there was celibacy. For hundreds of years this had been the rule for all serving soldiers until at the beginning of the third century, prolonged garrison duty made it unreasonable, but the tradition died hard, and it matched Martin's strong desire for sexual continence in the service of Christ.

Having taken these principles through his upbringing and military service into the very pores of his skin, Martin accepted them as the framework of his own spiritual life, and, later on, of the communities he was to bring into being. It is strange to think that western monasticism, with all its cultural triumphs, had its humble origin in the troubled cogitations of young Roman Christian soldiers.

Martin's baptism had taken place in AD 334 under the benevolent rule of an emperor who was determined that Christianity should become the imperial religion. Twenty-two years later, in AD 356, Martin found himself in a challenge face to face with a young pagan emperor, Julian, who was equally determined to put the clock back and restore the old Roman pagan gods to their rightful place. It resulted in his sudden departure from the army.

The twenty quiet years of military service for Martin were turbulent ones for the church as it began to discover the full implications of the changes which followed Constantine's dramatic conversion. Martin, though withdrawn in his mind from the world was still a member of the imperial guard, and therefore in touch with all the developments in church and state. Much of it was distasteful and irrelevant to him but he understood the main issues clearly, for when he emerged again into the limelight he knew exactly where he stood, and who to go to for guidance.

4

If Martin had, immediately after his baptism, been successful in fleeing from the world and found a lonely hermitage somewhere in the deserts of Egypt, he still would not have been able to escape from the all-pervading influence of that most remarkable of men, Flavius Valerius Constantinus, Constantine the Great. It is not given to many men or women suddenly and drastically to change the whole course of human history and to leave behind them traditions that still continue to rumble on nearly 2,000 years after they are dead, but such was Constantine. Martin's destiny was inextricably bound up with the lives of Constantine and his sons, whom he must have seen often in the course of his duties, and whose working vision of the church was to cause him much heart-searching.

In the year AD 306, ten years before Martin was born, Constantine, at the age of eighteen and in fear of his life, had galloped across the Roman roads of Britain to where his father, Constantius Chlorus lay dying at York. As he lay there Constantius commended his young son to the legions of Britain as his successor, and they duly acclaimed him as Caesar on 26 July. Under his leadership they then slowly

6   *A coin of Constantine I, obverse; 'to the Unconquerable Sun companion'*

made their way across Gaul, gathering as they went a great army of Gauls, Britons and barbarians. Constantine, with considerable political acumen for one so young, had to feel his way carefully, for when the emperor Diocletian had retired the power struggle for the succession had been bitterly contested.

On the eve of 28 October AD 312, Constantine found himself approaching Rome and a confrontation with the army of one of the rival contenders for the role of supreme Augustus, the Caesar Maxentius. Constantine was conscious of taking considerable risks, as his army was inferior in numbers, and might well have lost his nerve had he not had behind him the growing conviction that the gods were on his side. On his accession he had been granted a clear-cut religious conviction, which he felt could save and unite the empire in a way that Diocletian's *Genius populi Romani* could never have done. In his family tradition the worship of the Unconquerable Sun had always held a high place of honour, with its weekly festival of Sun-day; it had united his family, now it could unite the empire. Even the humblest slave in the fields, gazing at the glories of sunrise or sunset was moved by a sense of awe and wonder before this source of all life's blessings; and there was not any religion from the simplest to the most sophisticated that did not worship the sun as god under one name or another; as for the Christians, as far as he understood them it seemed as if they too gathered on the day of the sun to worship Christ as the Light of the World.

What happened next is confused, but both pagan and Christian historians of the time agree that Constantine received in answer to his spiritual preparations for the battle a dream or vision that left an indelible impact on him.[1]

> He was praying, he said, and God sent him a miraculous sign. It was after noon, and the sun was sinking on the horizon, when he saw, in the heavens above the sun, a luminous cross with this inscription attached, TOUTW NIKA (in this sign, conquer)

He did not understand the vision at first until the mysterious bishop Hosius of Cordova, a Spaniard in his entourage, explained it for him, but from then on he knew with certainty. The sign he had seen was the chi-rho, the secret symbol of the persecuted Christians. The God of the Unconquerable Sun he was so confident about, was none other than the God of the Christians, the eternal word made flesh, the Unconquerable Christ, the Light of Light.

He ordered that a jewelled replica of the sign be made and that a copy of the symbol should be immediately placed on all the standards of the legions. Thus armed, the whole army moved forward behind the symbol of the cross; Maxentius was defeated and Constantine at the head of his troops marched into Rome.

At first Constantine, now the sole ruler of the West, whilst his old rival and unwilling colleague Licinius ruled in the East, acted as the client of the Unconquerable Sun, blessed by the Christians' God. His coins were marked with a lifelike portrait of himself on one side and a dedication on the reverse to 'the Unconquerable Sun' with the cross added for good measure, perhaps by the excited devotion of Christian workers in the mint.[2] They were a reassurance to all the peoples of the empire of the new and happy era of gracious toleration for all worshippers of the gods. On 13 March AD 312 came the edict of toleration: 'it seemed to us that . . . the reverence paid to the Divinity merited our first and chief attention, and that it was proper that the Christians and all others should have liberty to follow that mode of religion, which to each of them appeared best'.[3] Six years later came the reassuring law to 'all judges, city people and craftsmen, that they should rest upon the venerable day of the Sun . . . with its venerable solemnities . . . a festal day.'[4] The lovers of the old gods of Rome and of the East, need fear no reprisals from this new emperor who supported the Christians so strongly and the Christians need take no offence, for though they usually called the day the Lord's day, and assembled on it for their worship, they had sometimes called it Sunday, as everyone else did.[5] It was an astute move, over which everyone rejoiced, and the Christians hardly seemed to notice that their new supporter, till the day of his death, remained Pontifex Maximus or High Priest of the old pagan religion at Rome.

It soon became clear, however, what Constantine was after; he wanted all the obvious benefits of Christianity with its close-knit organization and world-wide fellowship to strengthen and unite his empire. He observed its already sophisticated pastoral organization and knew that if he could win the loyalty of its leaders he would have a ready-made following throughout the empire that would give his rule a very stable foundation. There was too, another and more personal favour he wanted of the Christians; he had been told that free and total forgiveness was granted through baptism, and he was saving up for that on his deathbed, for his climb to the imperial throne had involved some very savage brutalities.

In AD 313, he exempted all ordained clergy from the onerous duty of acting as decurions in the municipalities, a compulsory office which had bankrupted many substantial people. So great was the rush of potential middle-class ordinands that seven years later he decreed that no one who had the means and position that qualified him to act as a decurion was to be ordained. He had learnt a sharp lesson, and corrupted many Christians in doing so. In 315, he granted to the clergy and church corporations the extraordinary largesse of exemption from the ordinary taxes, another law that was quickly repealed.

He went on to grant bishops the right to free slaves in the presence of their whole assembled congregation, whereas before the process had required the presence of the magistrate, an act which was the thin end of a very large wedge, which he continued to drive in during his reign. For people tended more and more to forsake the ordinary law courts for the often fairer decisions of the bishops, which apart from anything else were far less expensive, with the result that by the end of the century bishops often were the only magistrates operating.

The clergy were now supported by the state by regular revenues, through gifts of landed property and crop shares, which, in addition to the offerings of the new crowds of converts, made theirs a wealthy and important profession in society.[6] As the crowds now started to throng to Christian worship, the impoverished little house-churches of the persecution days were far too small. They were pulled down, and following the example of the emperor himself, who was denuding his coffers to build great temples and basilicas, many local townspeople built new basilicas. The liturgies, which before had been performed by the bishops, presbyters and deacons in the midst of groups of manageable size, and had ended up often with a love feast or dinner, became more and more distant and formalized, with the professional clergy as actors before a large and passive audience.

Problems, however, began quickly to assert themselves. The Christian church which had seemed such a united group under persecution was now seen to be seething with the most violent internal disagreements. Many of the new Christian clergy were place-seekers, and had become fascinated, like Constantine himself, by the pleasures of theological speculation; parties and power-groups were formed to promote this or that disputant, and the controversies, when it came down to which party owned the local basilica, or whose clergy were exempted from tax, or the decurionate, led to blows.

In order to restore law and order Constantine started to take matters into his own hands. In Africa, where a particularly violent disagreement between two parties had brewed up, he gave orders for his soldiery to move in, and in the fracas one of the congregation was killed and the bishop injured.[7] Controversies were becoming so widespread that by AD 325 Constantine took the momentous decision to call a council of as many bishops as could be mustered to the town of Nicaea, not far from the imperial palace of Nicomedia. He was determined that he would leave no stone unturned to secure a proper unity in this church on which he had pinned such hopes.

At state expense the emperor's carriages transported the 320 bishops and their entourages, numbering some 2,000 in all. Even as they rocked and bumped across the imperial roads, many of them quite simple and unlettered men, still bearing the scars of their tortures, and at least one a working shepherd from Cyprus, a subtle change was taking place in their status. From being humble local pastors for the most part, they were becoming court officials, even glorified civil servants, charged with letting their people know the emperor's will on their return. Government of the church by council and synod had come to stay and in the years that lay immediately ahead many of those present were to spend as much time in intrigue at court or attending synods as they did in the pastoral work of their parishes; the essential role of the bishop as local pastor was being finally buried.

At the time, however, it did not look like this, and they all came full of hope that their wrongs would be redressed and their disputes settled. Constantine had invited them all to send their complaints to him in advance. On the opening day he entered the conference hall with great dignity and took his seat as president. With his friends, bishop Hosius of Cordova and bishop Eusebius of Nicomedia seated on either side of him, he listened attentively to the opening speeches of welcome. He then produced from the folds of his robes a bundle of parchment rolls, which they clearly recognized as their lists of complaints. He ordered a brazier to be brought, and without a word deposited the whole lot in the flames. As they all watched, fascinated, they knew that they, the leaders of the universal church, were no longer free to argue as they had done before in often acrimonious, though open pursuit of theological truth, for a new element had entered with this unbaptized Christian emperor who was presiding over them, lecturing them, and quite insistent that before he would let them go, they were to give him and the church and empire at large a unanimous answer to the questions raised.

The main argument then revolved around the opinions of the presbyter Arius, of Alexandria, a gaunt and ungainly enthusiast who had been proclaiming in his church to a large and enthusiatic congregation that Jesus Christ was not from all eternity the Son of God, as one of the catchy verses he had composed to be sung went: 'There was a time when He was not.' Arius addressed the conference and to everyone's surprise sang one of his own songs. Present at the conference there stood a young man, also from Alexandria, who had come as deacon to the aged pope Alexander: a young man 'of lively manners and speech and of bright serene countenance'.[8]

He knew Arius only too well, and he set about thoroughly to discredit him, and to call for his condemnation. It was a remarkable, young man's performance, and many were swayed, in spite of the fact that they did not want to commit themselves one way or the other, feeling that any definition should leave as much room as possible for theological speculation. Athanasius was adamant on the grounds of biblical truth; to water down the main drift of the Scriptures was tantamount to rejecting them. In the end he won the day and so vigorous was the dynamic of his mind that it is the creed of Nicaea, declaring Jesus to be God of God, Light of Light, begotten of his Father before all worlds, that is sung in the churches today, whilst Arius' catchy little tune 'There was a time when he was not' is forgotten.

Constantine for once in his life was carried further than his better judgment wished to go, the moderates were stampeded, and poor Arius banished. The conference ended in euphoria, with a magnificent dinner presided over by Constantine at which he gave lavish presents to those who had pleased him. The Christians at Ticinum in northern

7 *Constantine the Great (drawn from a giant statue in the Capitoline Museum)*

Italy, might not know all the ins and outs or even the words of the new creed, but they knew, along with the rest of the world that a glorious victory had been won for Christ and his church, and that the great emperor had once again brought blessings on the Christian church.

The impressions of childhood are hard to efface and the small boy Martin, wedged in with the throng in the porch of the church, had known that there were certain words that meant blessing for the Church, like 'Nicaea' and 'catholic', and certain words that would always mean harm like 'Arius'.

In the inner councils of the church leaders, however, this was far from the case. For many, Nicaea had been a shameful defeat and no sooner had they returned home than they began the arguments again, with greater intensity. Many objected to the phrase Athanasius had insisted on, that Christ was of one substance (*homoousios*) with the Father; it was not biblical, it was misleading and anyway Athanasius was only a young deacon and an upstart. They found Constantine's ear and he listened. More councils were held, Athanasius, now bishop of Alexandria, was banished and Arius received an invitation to the court, though he died it was said in a public lavatory on the way.

In 337, Constantine having kept the feast of Easter in the great church of the apostles, the centrepiece of his new Rome, suitably named Constantine-city, or Constantinople, fell seriously ill and after being baptized, died in his white robe on 22 May 337 at the age of sixty-four. As he had lived so he died. The reading of his will was the signal for a chaos of intrigue and bloodshed, out of which his three sons, Constans, Constantius II and Constantine emerged as an uneasy triumvirate. Civil war broke out and in the end Constantius II became sole emperor after the pattern of his father. The barbarians, taking advantage of the constant threat of civil war, had been building up their forces on the banks of the Rhine and the Danube and at times had broken through, wreaking havoc where they went; they even camped outside Autun and marauding bands reached the suburbs of Rheims and Paris.[9]

Constantine's church which he had envisaged as a powerful unifying force only added to the confusion by becoming embroiled in a period of scandalous divisiveness, in which Constantius himself personally joined, to the shame of Christian people and the cynical amusement of the pagans. Constantius not only favoured Arius's teaching as his father was beginning to do before his death, but was determined to force it on the whole church by every means at his disposal. He nearly succeeded; old bishop Hosius, exiled to Pannonia, added his shaky signature to an Arian creed; the pope of Rome himself, Liberius, signed a formula which seemed to interpret Nicaea in an Arian way, and repudiated Athanasius; and as Jerome wrote afterwards 'The world groaned and was astonished to find itself Arian.'[10]

In all this bitter controversy one figure came to stand out as champion of the Nicene faith, both in the West and later, when he was exiled there, in the East. Hilary was a wealthy married man with one daughter, living in the town of Poitiers, when the people, seeking to establish a Christian church in the town persuaded him to be their bishop. He was devout and had quickly developed a skill in theology. As soon as he heard and read of the controversy over Athanasius and the Nicene creed, he grasped what many others had in different ways around him, that Arianism was not only untrue to the profundity of scriptural teaching, but led quickly to a spirit of worldliness and compromise. He saw too that Constantius's attempt to enforce Arianism on the church by physical threats, tortures and killings was totally alien to the spirit of Christianity. He had in the year AD 356 written an open letter to Constantius which had angered him and as a result he had been told to pack his bags in readiness for exile in Phrygia, where prison awaited him.

While this lone champion of the Catholic or Nicene cause was waiting to leave from Poitiers, Martin, at the age of forty, suddenly appeared at his house as if from nowhere, seeking guidance and instruction in how to pursue the spiritual life as a hermit in the desert.

Where he had been all this time must always remain unknown, but it would have been impossible for him not to have followed closely all that had been going on in spite of his determination to quit the world, for as soon as he reappears on the scene he has a clear understanding of the spiritual issues.

His leave-taking from the army had certainly been dramatic. A few years before, Constantius, unable alone to cope with the barbarian invasions, had appointed his young cousin Julian as a Caesar with the special task of restoring peace in Gaul, and Martin had found himself detailed to serve in this campaign under his command in the military unit attached to Julian's person.

Julian at this time was a remarkably successful and attractive young man, twenty-nine years of age. He had been eminently successful in conducting the campaign against almost insuperable odds, and was greatly admired in Gaul. Brought up at Constantius' court, he had been baptized after instruction from Arian teachers, but the posturing of the court bishops and laymen had revolted him and he had long been nurturing the plan to renege on his baptism and as soon as he received power to restore a refined form of the ancient worship of the Roman gods, in place of the official version of Christianity.

Flushed by his success he had started introducing the old pagan ways gently. When the *sacramenta* were made he had begun to have small ikons of the gods placed by the standards with incense burning before them, and the cross was quietly removed from them.[11] Martin was fully aware of what was happening, and, having arrived at the end of his term of years of service, decided to withdraw and make his way to the desert as he had longed to all his life; but he would go first to Hilary to express his admiration for his stand and to receive instruction from him in the spiritual life. He had, however, chosen an unfortunate moment to do this. Julian had won a great victory over the barbarians and was regrouping his forces on the left bank of the middle Rhine above Mayence in readiness to clean up the country as far as Cologne.

Julian and his guard had arrived near the city of Worms and had pitched camp. He decided in view of his recent success and the possibility of imminent battle to present donatives. These highly prized gold or silver ingots usually in the shape of a double axe head, were accompanied by gifts of coins, and were given to men who had given long and meritorious service.[12]

> As the barbarians were rushing within the two divisions of Gaul, Julian Caesar, bringing an army together at the city of the Vaugiones, began to distribute a donative to the soldiers. As was the custom in such a case, they were called forward one by one, until it came to the turn of Martin. Then, indeed, judging it a suitable opportunity for seeking his discharge – for he did not think it would be proper for him, if he were not to continue in the service, to receive a donative – he said to Caesar 'Hitherto I have served you as a soldier; allow me now to become a soldier to God; let the man who is to serve thee receive thy donative; I am the soldier of Christ; it is not lawful for me to fight.' Then truly the tyrant stormed on hearing such words, declaring that from fear of the battle, which was to take place on the morrow, and not from any religious feeling, Martin withdrew from the service. But Martin, full of courage . . . exclaims: 'If this conduct of mine is ascribed to cowardice and not to faith, I will take my stand unarmed before the line of battle to-morrow, and in the name of the Lord Jesus, protected by the sign of the cross, and not by shield or helmet, I will safely penetrate the ranks of the enemy.' He is ordered therefore, to be thrust back into prison, determined on proving his words true by exposing himself unarmed to the barbarians. But, on the following day, the enemy sent ambassadors to treat about peace and surrendered both themselves and all their possessions. In these circumstances who can doubt that this victory was due to the saintly man?[13]

To Julian with his sardonic attitude towards Christianity, such a dramatic pose as a potential martyr by an old officer who was due for retirement anyway had a strong element of farce. Julian was making no martyrs; rather he intended, as soon as he was in a position to do so, to restore to the clergy the two Christian privileges that he felt they so sadly lacked, humility and holy poverty. He would ban them from his court, withdraw their growing privileges as magistrates, remove all their tax concessions and grants, bring back from exile all who had been banned from their homes on religious grounds, and make any who had had the impudence to destroy heathen temples restore them at their own expense.[14]

Martin's action, however, had about it an eerie sense of mystery that struck deep chords, not only in Julian's but in every Gallic mind; for, whether Martin realized it or not, this was his first introduction to the Celtic people as their particular apostle. He had acted as a new-style Druid of Christ, for to stand between contending armies and to establish peace between them was one of the Druid's special functions.[15] To see Martin's offer made and accepted in public in such circumstances and to experience its result was, to say the least, remarkable.

Martin was free at last from those chains which had bound him to the army in the service of the emperor Constantine and his family for so long. As he stepped from the prison into the light of day, it was with a sense of liberation that only those know who have been set free at last from a partly congenial task to do what they have longed for all their lives. It was high summer, and to be free, and walking steadily along the straight roads, with his knapsack on its forked stick over his shoulder, towards Poitiers, Hilary, a hermitage and heart's desire, was as much as any man could need to make him supremely happy, especially when he was forty years of age and at the beginning of his life's real work.

Part Two

Hermit

From a long way off Martin could see as he approached, the town of the Pictavi, nowadays known as Poitiers, standing some 130 feet high above the surrounding plain on a plateau, a small, fortified Roman town. Entering the town he had to cross the little river Clain, which ran around the foot of its cliffs, a stream that was to provide the background to ten of the happiest years of his life. He walked on through the streets, past the shrines, baths and the amphitheatre, until on the slopes of the east side of the town he found the church, the bishop's house, and the baptistery, the last of which miraculously stands to this day, enlarged over the years, but with vestiges of its original baptismal basin – the oldest surviving Christian building in France.

The bishop's house, into which he was welcomed, was pervaded by an atmosphere of strict religious discipline, and for the first time in his life Martin must have experienced in its quietness something of the reality of the religious stillness he sought, but had so far been unable to create around himself.

Hilary was the first bishop of Poitiers, and, as was becoming quite common at this period, conducted his parish, with the aid of a small group of presbyters or deacons – the brothers[1] – who lived in the house with him and shared his life, along with his wife and daughter Abra. All were dedicated to the life of the *conversi*, to fasting, scripture-reading and meditation, and had committed themselves to a life of sexual continence; in the same sort of way as bishop Eusebius of Vercellae: 'though living in the city, they observed the monastic institute, and with the government of his church united the sobriety of an ascetic life.'[2]

In this household Martin was immediately at home. After his first dash for freedom he had found at Poitiers, as he had hoped, one who would challenge him to serve Christ in his church in new ways, and

43

help to direct him from a position of great spiritual authority. Hilary was certainly the right man to present him with this challenge. He was an active parish pastor, with a widening sphere of influence, who had been condemned for his outspokenness by the emperor Constantius to an exile of unspecified time; and when Martin arrived he was waiting with his bags packed for the imperial confirmation of his time of departure and its destination. He may well have felt that the end of his useful ministry had come, but in point of fact he was on the threshold of a brilliant writing career, which was to lead to his being acclaimed as one of the four Latin fathers of the church for all ages to come. In his exile in Phrygia he was to gain fresh insights into the subtleties of theology from eastern theologians, and was to discover in himself how to use his gifts of clear exposition not only in prose but in lyrical poetry.

But now, though a few of his parish addresses had already been published, he was here talking freely, and Martin heard unravelled that mystery that was to become the devotional core of Gallic Christianity, the doctrine of the Holy Trinity, the three persons in one God. He heard tell, with a clarity of expression, of the Incarnation of the eternal Word in the person of Jesus, which the local bishops of his experience had only been able to state baldly as revealed truth, plain and unadorned. Above all he learnt of the dangers of the imperial favours of the house of Constantine to the church, stated with a vehemence that pleased him after his recent brush with authority; how the rash of church buildings, the crowds seeking baptism and the corruption of the new style church leaders pledged to the search for compromise, were wrecking the church as if by the design of the Devil or Satan; for Arianism was rampant and it meant worldliness, place-hunting and untruth.

It is easy to visualize the groups of listening brothers and sisters around Hilary as the words, throbbing with vitality, took shape in the dialogue in the bishop's house at Poitiers, to be written down a few years later and sent to Constantius:[3]

> What then is the character of the persecution of Constantius?
> We fight against a persecutor who tries to receive us,
> against a foe who ever offers us blandishments, against
> Constantius the Antichrist. He does not proscribe us that we
> should be deprived of our lives but he endows us that we
> may gain spiritual death. He does not crush out our life by
> imprisonment and so give us liberty, but he gives us posts
> of honour in the palace which bring us into bondage. . . . I
> say to thee, Constantius, what I would have said to Nero,
> what Decius and Maximianus would have heard from me.

It is against God you fight, against His Church you rage,
you persecute His saints, you hate those who preach Christ,
you take away true religion.

It was heady stuff from one who had no doubt spotted the features
of the imperial face gazing down on the worshippers from the great
paintings in the new basilicas of the triumphant Christ in glory.

If Martin was carried away, Hilary in his turn was delighted that
at this eleventh hour, an officer of the imperial guard had been by
Divine providence sent to him, and one who seemed so apt to learn
and to espouse his cause. Feeling that here was one to whom he
could entrust the management of his new congregation and who
would be able to speak with authority for the 'cause', he approached
Martin and persuaded him to receive ordination as deacon at his
hands.[4] He then went on to try by repeated encouragements to bind
him more closely to himself by ordaining him as a member of his
team of presbyters, but at this Martin jibbed: the thought of becoming
more and more involved in the affairs and internal politics of the
local church appalled him, apart from his own quite proper sense of
unworthiness.

Hilary realized, however, that even if he had not gained one who
would help to care for his parish in his absence, he had certainly
found one who would speak up for the 'cause' in the wider context of
Gaul, for it so happened around this time that, with the constant
demands made on bishops to attend at court or at councils, the custom
had been quickly growing of a bishop sending one of his deacons,
especially authorized with 'letters commendatory' to speak for him
at councils and elsewhere. Athanasius had shown at Nicaea how well
a deacon could present his bishop's case, and the Council of Sardica
had given formal approval to the custom by laying down that if a
bishop wished to send a petition to court or to his metropolitan, he
should do so by sending one of his deacons.[5] Hilary had found someone who would not be afraid of courts and courtly men, if he could
persuade him to act for him.

At the same time, however, he had discovered with penetrating
insight a deeper quality in Martin than just the ability to stand up for
catholic truth in the anvil-ding of church controversy. Martin had
opened to him his increasing sense that the trouble lay not so much
in the area of controversy, but in a deeper realm of the spirit, where
the source of all evil himself had to be faced, the Devil or Satan, and
he spoke to Hilary of his lifelong interest in the work of the exorcists
in their struggle with those who had been possessed by Satan, the
pathetic *energoumenoi* who shared the porch with the catechumens.
Hilary therefore appointed him an exorcist. Although at this time the

role of the exorcist was becoming more and more stylized into that of a minor functionary who had the unenviable task of caring for the *energoumenoi* in and out of church, and of helping in the baptism service by marking the ever-increasing flow of catechumens and candidates for baptism with the sign of the cross, it still retained on occasion, as here, its more primitive concept. Originally the ordination of an exorcist had been the means whereby the bishop in the presence of the whole worshipping community had declared publicly that one of the members of the congregation had been given the charisma of healing for casting out devils; a charisma that had been proved by already demonstrated power; for it was 'a spiritual function which comes direct from God, and manifests itself by results'.[6]

As a result of his stay with Hilary, Martin was now a soldier of Christ, suitably armed with spiritual weapons and authority, and ready to start his campaign against the foe; he only awaited his marching orders. He did not have to wait long, for, the second time in his life, Martin had a dream with a clear message; in it he was being told to undertake a most unlikely journey of over 1,000 miles right across Europe to visit his parents and to seek their conversion. From whatever deep springs of personal motivation this dream sprang, Hilary, on being told of it was left in no doubt about its interpretation. It all fitted in to make a clear picture of the Divine guidance. Hilary himself was leaving as a prisoner for exile in Phrygia; Hilary's agent Martin, was being directed right into the heart of the headquarters of the Arian heresy, for within six months or so the emperor Constantius' court was to forgather at Sirmium in Pannonia, to plan the final campaign, under the able leadership of the two young courtier bishops Ursacius and Valens, to force the Arian doctrine upon the universal Church.

So, after a short stay at Poitiers, Martin 'set forth in accordance with the expressed wish of the holy Hilarius, and, after being adjured by him with many prayers and tears, that he would in due time return.'[7] Suddenly to find himself one early autumn morning on the road again, after saying farewell to the little band of good companions and their leader, who had received him with such charitable hospitality and prudent advice, filled Martin with depression. Apart from anything else, the length of the journey ahead of him in winter must have appalled even this intrepid marcher, trained to marching for sixteen miles a day in full armour and laden with camping equipment. Two things, however, comforted him; first he was walking alone, and then, he had his 'letters commendatory' from Hilary in his knapsack.

The next best thing to a cell for a hermit, is to walk alone. Martin loved to stare at the sky, to watch the formation of clouds;[8] he took in everything as he went along, sheep, farm workers, the state of the cultivation of fields, and the flight of birds for he was an ardent bird watcher; and all these things would come out spontaneously in his teaching later.[9] There was, however, one aspect of the landscape that could not fail to force itself upon his notice, and at the same time provide a kind of overture to his impending struggle with Satan, for everywhere he went, every village through which he passed, by every spring and rivulet, on every prominent hilltop that came in sight; wherever there was sign of human habitation there were the shrines. They were a constant reminder of the supremacy of Rome – roadside altars, temples, some large and pretentious and some small with their collection of pitiful offerings beside them. The inscriptions that he found everywhere came to him now in his loneliness with a monotonous frequency that built up into active repulsion at the names, Jupiter, Minerva, Mercury, names that were coming to rankle in his mind as symbols of the ubiquitous presence of Satan, with whom he had set out to do single combat in Christ's name.

Though he walked alone gladly, Martin, like any travelling Christian, was glad of the document in his haversack that bound him not only with Hilary and his congregation, but with his fellow Christians everywhere. No travelling Christian in the church at this time and for the previous centuries would dream of setting out on a journey without 'letters pacifical' if he were a layman, or 'letters commendatory' if he were a clergyman.[10] These letters were one of the wonders of the ancient world both to the Christian and pagan alike, for they admitted the bearer, even though he were a slave, into a world-wide community of hospitality, the like of which had never been seen before. They explained who the bearer was and his or her purpose in travelling, they commended the Christian church wherever the traveller found himself, to welcome him hospitably as a fellow communicant, and, more remarkably, if he were poor, asked for food and shelter for him, and finally the documents themselves were marked with the bishop's own personal seal to ensure that they were not forgeries.

Yet as Martin took pleasure in the thought of his 'letters commendatory' safely stowed in his knapsack, a pass into the hearts and homes of all catholic Christians and supporters of Hilary, he also knew that they would bring down on his head a torrent of abuse and rejection and possibly physical violence from Arian congregations.

He trudged on for mile after mile along the almost deserted roads with nothing but scrub and forest, a grim and steady climb up on to the Massif central, and the gradual appearance of the mountains of the Puy de Dome with the hated shrine of Mercury visible for miles from the top. Beyond lay Lyons, capital city of the Gauls, where the first martyrs of Gaul had suffered a most violent death in the amphitheatre as long ago as AD 177, before the representatives of all the

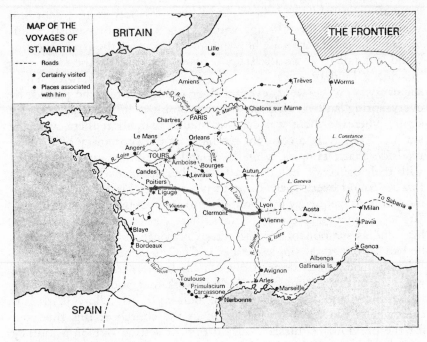

MAP OF THE VOYAGES OF ST. MARTIN
- - - - Roads
* Certainly visited
• Places associated with him

BRITAIN

THE FRONTIER

Lille
Amiens
Trèves
Worms
R. Seine
R. Marne
Chalons sur Marne
Chartres
PARIS
L. Constance
Le Mans
Orleans
Angers
R. Loire
TOURS
Amboise
Bourges
Autun
Candes
Levraux
L. Geneva
Poitiers
Liguge
R. Vienne
Lyon
To Sabaria
R. Loire
Clermont
Vienne
Aosta
Milan
Pavia
Blaye
R. Rhone
R. Isere
Bordeaux
Genoa
Albenga
Gallinaria Is.
R. Garonne
Avignon
Toulouse   ?
Primulacium
Carcassonne
Arles
Marseille
Narbonne
SPAIN

8 *The voyages of St Martin*

Gallic tribes, at their annual assembly, held every August with their Roman conquerors. The production of his 'letters commendatory' here would have greatly encouraged many Christians who felt they were on the threshold of a new testing with the growing imperial enforcement of Arian doctrines.

From there he climbed on up into the Alps, through, it would seem, the traditional little St Bernard Pass, and whether because of the snow or not he lost himself among the trackways, though he could hardly have missed the shrine of Jupiter that crowned the mountain of the pass.[11]

He fell into the hands of robbers. And when one of them lifted up his axe and poised it above Martin's head, another of them met with his right hand the blow as it fell; nevertheless, having had his hands bound behind his back, he was handed over to one of them to be guarded and stripped. The robber, having led him to a private place apart from the rest, began to enquire of him who he was. Upon this, Martin replied that he was a Christian. The robber next asked him whether he was afraid. Martin most courageously replied that he never before had felt so safe . . . he added

he grieved rather for the man in whose hands he was. . . .
then, entering on a discourse concerning evangelical truth,
he preached the word of God to the robber. The robber
believed; and, after expressing his respect for Martin, he
restored him to the way, entreating him to pray to the
Lord for him. That same robber was afterwards seen leading
a religious life; so that, in fact, the narrative I have given
above is based on an account furnished by himself.

After this hair-raising episode, Martin moved down into the lush
green plains of northern Italy, and passed through the imperial city
of Milan, where in the imperial precincts he met his adversary Satan
for the first time: 'the devil met him in the way, having assumed the
form of a man'.[12]

The devil first asked him to what place he was going, Martin
having answered him to the effect that he was minded to
go whithersoever the Lord called him, the devil said to
him: 'Wherever you go, or whatever you attempt, the
devil will resist you.' Then Martin, replying to him said:
'The Lord is my helper; I will not fear what man can do
unto me.' Upon this his enemy immediately vanished out
of his sight.

The imagery here is not that of the sometimes ludicrous descriptions
in the medieval hagiographies, where Cernunnos, the horned god of
the Celts had become besmirched into an imaginary monster; here it
is a case of the much subtler concept of the gods of antiquity. According to the universal awareness of all classes in the ancient world, if a
god wished to communicate with men or women, he or she must
disguise themselves by taking over temporarily some human being
or animal without them being even aware of it.
So Homer writes that when the goddess Aphrodite wished to
rouse Helen's love for Paris,[13]

she went to summon Helen. She found Helen on the high
tower, surrounded by Trojan women. Aphrodite put out
her hand, plucked at her robe and spoke to her in the
disguise of an old woman she was very fond of, a wool-
worker who used to make beautiful wool for her when
she lived in Lacedaimon. 'Come,' said the goddess, mimick-
ing this woman, 'Paris wants you to go home with him.'
Helen was perturbed and looked at the goddess. When
she beheld the beauty of her neck and her lovely breasts and
sparkling eyes, she was struck with awe,

So too at Caesarea Philippi, Jesus had addressed his close companion Peter who was trying to turn him back from the cross, with 'Get behind me, Satan.'

It is very significant that Hilary's Antichrist, Constantius, was himself about to move from Milan to Rome, and then on to Pannonia, the same destination as Martin, with a view to putting the finishing touches there to his campaign for Arianizing Christianity. Whether the man of Satan's choice was an imperial guard who recognized Martin, and was trying to warn him, will never be known, but this confrontation marked the first round of a long and desultory battle, destined to go on all his life in which Satan became a personality almost as well known to Martin as Christ himself. Martin eventually arrived in Sabaria in the early summer, and he had the joy of seeing his mother and many of her neighbours enrolled as catechumens, though his father held out stubbornly and refused to believe. Only 250 miles away at Sirmium, the emperor Constantius arrived with his entourage, completely composed of able, Arianizing diplomat-bishops. In the autumn of AD 357 they persuaded the aged bishop Hosius of Cordova to sign a statement which was to be sent to all bishops for signature, to the effect that the very Council of Nicaea at which he had been vice-chairman, and whose creed he had so vigorously supported was no longer valid. With the pope of Rome, Liberius, in exile having signed a similar statement, and many of the loyal bishops also in exile, it seemed as if the wishes of Constantius had been fulfilled.

It is almost inconceivable that Martin himself did not go to Sirmium, for the whole countryside was in a furore. If he did not, other catholics did, as those who received short shrift from Germinius the Arian bishop of Sirmium show.[14]

> A layman called Heraclian was brought before him: 'It is Eusebius (of Vercellae) and Hilary who have put these ideas into your head,' he said, and as Heraclian tried to defend himself Germinius said: 'see what a long tongue he has. You will not be able to break his teeth'. Immediately a deacon and a reader flew at the accused and struck him in the face. . . . At the end of the audience, the clergy of Germinius spoke of indicting the dissentients before the governor and demanding their heads.

In this kind of atmosphere, Martin received the full treatment on the production of his 'letters commendatory': 'almost single handed, he was fighting most strenuously against the treachery of the priests, and had been subjected to many punishments (for he was publicly scourged, and at last was compelled to leave the city)'. He was not cut out for this kind of peculiar fighting over catchwords, and had the sense to withdraw and make his way back to Milan.

Milan, or Mediolanum as it was known in the days of the empire, was a thriving city, the first in importance in Italy after Rome itself. The emperors had created it a city of imperial residence and at this period it was growing rapidly in importance. The court poet Ausonius describes the grand buildings, and the long marble colonnades surmounted with statues where the citizens were free to walk from the Golden Palace, the imperial residence where the peace of the church had been declared, to the extensive baths of Hercules. All roads from Gaul, Rome and the East met here, and in these days of crisis in church and state, there were constant comings and goings of diplomats, agents and soldiers of all races.[15]

A brilliant society had grown up around the court, where philosophy, religion and literature were taken seriously, not only in the court but in the homes and stately country villas around. To add lustre to it all, the emperor had recently dismissed the uninspiring bishop Dionysius, an obstinate adherent of the Nicene faith, and had appointed in his place his own nominee, Auxentius, the distinguished Arian theologian from the East; a brilliant and peaceable man, who in other circumstances would have been well suited to the people of Milan. But controversy was the order of the day, as Gregory of Nyssa describes the feel of it in a city elsewhere:[16]

> the clothes-vendors, the money-lenders, the victuallers.
> Ask about pence and he will discuss the Generate and the
> Ingenerate. Enquire the price of bread, he answers; Greater
> is the Father, and the Son is subject. Say that a bath would
> suit you, and he defines that the Son is made out of nothing.

Martin arrived into this highly charged atmosphere exhausted; he was being driven by force of circumstance to take the battle where he knew in his heart of hearts it was to be fought out, in the hermit's cell. He was sure that Satan would appear there and could be faced and defeated in single combat with all the armoury of Christ, away from the web of conflicting motivations that go to make up the wordiness of theological controversy; so in the city he founded a hermitage, or monastery.

By this time Martin had become cautious in choosing to whom he should show his 'letters commendatory'. He would certainly not go to the church of Auxentius and produce them there, and as the catholics had been deprived of their place of worship he must needs go and hunt for them around the city, where they were meeting for worship in one another's houses or out in the fields, ministered to by the catholic presbyter, Philaster.[17] He found the church in the two divisions of Gaul in a distracted condition through the departure of Hilary into exile, and no doubt because of his being known as Hilary's deacon, his little monastery was besieged by pilgrims from all over Gaul. One event of great importance to his life, however, occurred here, which was to have a profound effect both on his life and on the lives of many other devout Christians. The great Catholic champion Athanasius, in exile in the desert, had gathered together material to write a life of the father of all hermits, Antony of Egypt, and the book was published during the year or so when Martin was at Milan. It was a book that was eagerly devoured by catholic Christians throughout the world and possessed a strange converting power. Twenty years later, after it had been circulating for some time, Augustine was to describe its effect.[18]

> There was a monastery at Milan, outside the city walls, full of good brothers, of whom Ambrose was the foster father; yet we had never heard of it. Pontitianus went on talking, and we listened in silence. So he was led to tell us how once he and three of his comrades at Trèves – the Emperor being detained at the afternoon games in the circus – went out for a stroll in the gardens beneath the city walls; how they parted company, two going off by themselves; how these two entered aimlessly into a house wherein dwelt certain of thy servants, men poor in spirit, of whom is the kingdom of heaven, and found there a volume containing the life of Antony. One of them began to read, and as he read his soul caught fire, so that then and there he began to think of plunging into the monastic life.

Martin, on reading it, would undoubtedly like the two young men, and indeed Augustine and thousands of others at the time had been quite overpowered by its message, and simply waited for the first opportunity to make their first visit into the desert. One senses that it was almost a relief when bishop Auxentius heard of Martin's activity, and bitterly persecuted him; 'and, after he had assailed him with many injuries, violently expelled him from the city.'[19] With him fled one of the much venerated presbyters of the city, motivated perhaps like himself to get away from the bitterness of controversy, after reading Antony's life. They started walking towards Poitiers, not this time across the Alps, but by the long way along the coast road, until they came to the town of Albenga, a town on which Constantius had lavished his generosity, and therefore in all probability, a town under Arian dominance. Dejected at the thought of any further din of controversy, they looked out to sea and saw the deserted island of Gallinaria, with its screeching gulls. Here they went and recreated the Egyptian situation as near as they could, and Martin started the longed for hermit's life in earnest.

In the world they left behind the controversy rumbled on. The state vehicles trundling over the long, straight roads, full of bishops for this or that synod or council, became a standing joke, and in the end the intrepid Gallic bishops of 'our part of the world', faithful to the teaching of Nicaea, Athanasius and Hilary, in spite of the pope of Rome's defection, jibbed, and proudly declined to travel at the public expense.[20] When at last the bishops met for the consecration of the great basilica of St Stephen at Constantinople in AD 360, Constantius had had his way, or so it seemed: 'the world groaned and awoke to find itself Arian'. as Jerome described it. Then suddenly Constantius was dead, and the whole Christian world found to its alarm that it now had a serious-minded, ascetic young emperor in Julian, brilliant in the wars and a baptized Christian, but who came to the throne disgusted with Christianity and its perpetual bickering and was determined to restore the old paganism of his forefathers in all its stately glory. How he set about it, and the reactions of the Christian people were of no consequence to the two lonely men on the island of Gallinaria, who were living roughly on roots and what the wild land had to offer them.

6

There I sat solitary, full of bitterness; my disfigured limbs shuddered away from the sackcloth, my dirty skin was taking on the hue of the Ethiopian's flesh: every day tears, every day sighing, and if in spite of my struggles sleep would tower over and sink upon me, my battered body ached on the naked earth. Of food and drink I say nothing, since even a sick monk uses only cold water, and to take anything cooked is wanton luxury. Yet that same I, who for fear of hell condemned myself to such a prison, I, the comrade of scorpions and wild beasts, was there, watching the maidens in their dances: my face haggard with fasting, my mind burnt with desire in my frigid body, and the fires of lust alone leaped before a man prematurely dead. So, destitute of all aid, I used to lie at the feet of Christ, watering them with my tears, wiping them with my hair, struggling to subdue my rebellious flesh with seven days' fasting. I grew to dread even my cell, with its knowledge of my imaginings; and grim and angry with myself, would set out solitary to explore the desert: and wherever I would spy the depth of a valley or a precipitious rock, there was the place of my prayer, there the torture house of my unhappy flesh: and the Lord himself is witness, after many tears, and eyes that cling to heaven, I would sometimes seem to myself to be one with the angelic hosts.[1]

That was not Martin: even if he felt like it, as he probably did on Gallinaria, he could never have expressed himself so fluently. It was written by a fellow Pannonian, slightly younger than himself, Jerome, who at the age of twenty-seven left the comforts of Rome to try out the hermit's life for himself in a cave in the Syrian desert. There is a compelling romance about the hermit's life, and in the age of Martin and Jerome it had for multitudes an irresistible fascination in spite of the fact that the day to day reality of it could be so frightening. What made it so compelling was that it was a way of life that had grown out of the harsh experience of the early Christian communities in the days of persecution and still provided a way for devout Christians to identify with them.

Many Christians were sickened by what had happened in the fifty or so years of the peace of the church; what had started out as such a glorious triumph full of promise had gone sour, and the church was in danger of becoming a parody of Christianity. The quality that was lacking was that provided by the constant threat of persecution, which implied all the time that being a Christian could at any moment mean deprivation of personal goods, job, reputation and could even mean the death penalty. As Kierkegaard had noted: 'without risk, faith is an impossibility. To be related to spirit means to undergo a test',[2] and for three centuries the test had been martyrdom. Many had even expressed their longing to undergo torture, and public disgrace and not to give in because as the pain of it slowly receded, and the noise of the shouting had died away, there would be Christ himself with the crown of victory for his aching servant. The hermit and ascetic, as he made his cell of palm leaves or entered his cold cave, considered that he was about to endure a 'white martyrdom', a martyrdom that he was prepared to endure for a long time in order to gain the same crown as those who had spilt their red blood in a moment.

Many who started failed and returned home to the world, for it was no child's play; but most returned having learnt something about God and themselves. Jerome was one of these; he stuck to his hermit's cell in the desert for six years. To alleviate the boredom he persuaded a local rabbi to teach him Hebrew, a skill that enabled him a few years later, when he had returned to the world, to begin to translate the scriptures into contemporary Latin straight from the Hebrew – a translation that came to be known as the Vulgate, the support of millions of Christians for many centuries. During those years he too had caught at first hand the spirit of the desert and what made this most unlikely place so exciting for Christians. One of his own favourite works was the booklet which he wrote on the life of Paul, the first hermit. It was the kind of story told in the churches of Martin's childhood and there are few who cannot sense something of the excitement of the discovery of the joy of religious solitude that pulsates through it:[3]

> The boy Paul – he was then fifteen years of age – took flight
> to the mountains, there to wait while the persecution ran

its course. What had been his necessity became his free
choice. Little by little he made his way, sometimes turning
back and again returning, till at length he came upon a rocky
mountain, and at its foot, at no great distance, a huge cave,
its mouth closed by a stone. There is a thirst in men to pry
into the unknown; he moved the stone, and eagerly explor-
ing came within on a spacious courtyard open to the sky,
roofed by the wide-spreading branches of an ancient palm,
and with a spring of clear shining water; a stream ran
hasting from it and was soon drunk again, through a
narrow opening. . . . So then, in this beloved habitation,
offered to him as it were by God Himself, he lived his life
through in prayer and solitude; the palm-tree provided
him with food and clothing.

The book, however, that really shook Christendom was the life of
Antony the Great, written by Athanasius, and published whilst
Martin was at Milan, in AD 357. Here was the authentic biography
of the master of the life of Christian solitude himself, and it summed
up for the general reader its most appealing facets. Born of wealthy
parents in the year AD 251 at Heracleopolis in Middle Egypt, Antony
went to church with them on Sundays. One Sunday he heard the
words of the gospel read; 'If thou wilt be perfect, go, sell what thou
hast, and give to the poor and come follow me, and thou shalt have
treasure in heaven.'
He left home and lived rough at first in the fields on the edge of
the village; after a time he moved off into the desert and settled in a
deserted tomb. After fifteen years in search of deeper solitude, he
went on with a supply of six months' bread in a sack and found a
ruined castle with a spring beside it. For twenty years he lived there,
fighting devils real and imaginary, and facing the insistent demands
of his flesh. At the end of it he found himself surrounded by people
of all ages who had fled to him for shelter from the horrors of Diocletian's persecution.
Hearing of the persecution Antony saw his chance of 'red martyrdom' and went down immediately to Alexandria to minister to the
confessors in prison who were awaiting the death sentence. Ignored
by the persecutors he retreated once again into the desert, not to the
castle which he felt was too overcrowded, but, wandering on, he at
last found an almost inaccessible spot at the foot of a mountain by
the shores of the Red Sea; the ideal refuge, a stream of clear gushing
water and some uncultivated palm trees. Armed with a spade, a
mattock, and some corn he cultivated a little plot and planted herbs
so as to give refreshment to any who found him and not to be a

burden on anyone. Only once could he be enticed away, and that was by the horror of Arianism and its worldliness, and on this account he went on a highly successful preaching foray to Alexandria, where he warned everyone: 'the Church is on the point of being given up to men who are like senseless beasts. For I saw the Lord's house and mules standing round it on all sides in a ring, and kicking the things therein, just like a herd kicks when it leaps in confusion.'[4]

Antony was a solitary, and though disciples came out in droves to find him and camp by him, he managed in the end to shake them all off and to carry on his spiritual warfare alone; it is doubtful even if for years at a time he ever attended a church service or received the sacraments. Today when one reads the extraordinary story, it is difficult not to be perplexed at this mystery of a man who left the world as completely as he knew how; and in doing so laid the foundations of a great new culture, for out of the confusion of the many solitaries in their huts and caves in the deserts of Egypt and Syria grew the monasteries that were to keep the quality of Christian life and culture fresh during the ravages of the Dark Ages.

It was in the spirit of Saint Antony and fired by his example that Martin and his presbyter colleague stepped ashore on Gallinaria, their imaginations stirred by the thought of Antony's hermitage on the mountainside by the shores of the Red Sea. What Martin had not bargained for was that whilst a gushing spring, a few dates, and a handful of wheat grain may be all very well to sustain a quiet life in the Egyptian desert, on the northern shores of the Mediterranean it is much colder and bodily needs become that much more demanding. For two years Martin lived on roots and became so physically exhausted that when his friend called round to see him to tell him his master Hilary had been freed from exile, he found him barely recovered from a nearly fatal dose of the root of the plant hellebore – the Christmas rose – a cure for worms which as an old eighteenth-century physician wrote: 'where it killeth not the patient; it would certainly kill the worms.'[5]

Martin came out of his solitude to return to the world a wiser man in one way especially; he had seen the stark terror of physical suffering borne alone. It was one thing to die a martyr in the open arena surrounded by fellow human beings, however hostile; it was terrifying to be dying alone, secretly and racked with pain and no human being in sight to care about it or share it. He never rejected human companionship again. He had emerged chastened by his experiences and in desperate need of dialogue with Hilary, his spiritual guide.

Rumour had it that Hilary had landed at Rome. Martin marched there first, and finding him already gone, doggedly retraced his steps along the coast road, the way Christianity had first entered Gaul, and at last found Hilary at home at Poitiers, resting and planning with indomitable courage, how best to rally the forces of the Gallic church against Arianism. It was not altogether surprising that after hearing Martin's report, Hilary set out with the startlingly simple project of ousting Auxentius from Milan and restoring the catholic clergy and congregations to their churches.

Before he went, however, he had settled Martin near Poitiers in surroundings that were to provide the background to the ten happiest and most creative years of his life.

7

When, early in the year of AD 361, Martin entered once more into the bishop's house at Poitiers, the two friends had changed and matured. Hilary, from being the naïve and vital rallier to a good cause, had matured intellectually into a theologian of world-wide repute, with some widely read and admired books behind him. Exile in Phrygia and the opportunity of meeting and exchanging ideas with many of the able theologians and leaders of the churches of the East, had confirmed for him intellectually what he had grasped before intuitively.

Among the many bishops he had met whilst at the fateful Council of Seleucia was one Eustathius, bishop of Sabaste. This strange and dynamic character, was like himself an exile from his parish. A clergyman's son, in his youth he had visited the Thebaïd where many of the Egyptian monks had settled, and after a chequered career had become an acknowledged authority on the ascetics of the desert. Even at this very time he was counselling a young man Basil, later to become bishop of Caesarea, in the formation of a corporate monastic rule, which was to form the basis of all rules of monasteries in the churches of the East.

From people such as this Hilary had learnt, during his absence, much more about the various forms of the solitary and community life which were developing in the deserts, so that when Martin, whose stature too had grown from his recent experience, spoke about the future, he was ready to encourage him in wide-ranging discussion. It is possible to trace the nature of that discussion from what happened next, for Hilary provided Martin with the ruin of a villa in the country which he possessed near Poitiers, in which to live as a hermit, with the understanding that if any followers came to join him he would not reject them but start to form them into some kind of monastery; and with Martin's background that could only mean one largely coloured by his experience as an officer in the Roman army.

Hilary's country villa, thirteen kilometres from Poitiers, had been demolished by the invasion of the Alemanni in AD 276, and never repaired. It stood a few yards from a 'clear rushing stream', the upper reaches of the river Clain; there was a patch nearby for the cultivation of herbs, and all that was needed for self-support was a 'spade and a mattock and some corn'. The central feature of the ruin was a large cavern with a dry concrete floor, which had at one time possibly been a grain store; and dotted about on the cliff-like hills that rose on either side of the valley were natural caves, so that the whole scene was reminiscent on a small and intimate scale, and in a green-Gallic way, of the Thebaïd and the desert valleys on the banks of the river Nile; where Antony's followers dwelt.

The villa and the community that grew up round about it came to be called Locociacum, the place of the little cells, or Ligugé,[1] from the familiar desert-style circle of huts, to be reflected later in countless similar Celtic communities in Britain and Ireland. The foundations of the site have recently been excavated so that it is possible to trace how the rooms of the villa lay, and to stand in a part of the great cave that Martin found when he arrived.

Martin came to the ruins in the spring of AD 361, and set up his quarters there. He was to stay there untroubled by the world's affairs for the next ten years, the happiest and most creative period of his life – a period to which he always afterwards looked back longingly as the peak of his spiritual powers. He was very soon joined, as seems almost to have been planned, by a group of brothers. There is little indication as to how they lived, but it could well have been like those in the Nitrian desert, who lived their own individual lives in their cells or caves, occupying themselves in prayer, reading and the making of mats, and all gathering together for some form of worship on Sundays. Martin himself was available for consultation, for soon 'a certain catechumen joined him, being desirous of becoming instructed in his doctrines and discipline'.[2]

This catechumen was to play a decisive if passive role in Martin's future, for Martin, by raising him to life from his deathbed, established such a reputation for himself that he immediately became placed in the popular Christian mind on a par with the apostles themselves, and as a veritable Christian Druid by the pagans.[3]

> After the lapse of only a few days, the catechumen, seized with a langour, began to suffer from a violent fever. It so happened that Martin had then left home, and having remained away three days, he found on his return that life had departed from the catechumen; and so suddenly had death occurred, that he had left this world without receiving

baptism. The body being laid out in public was being honoured by the last sad offices on the part of the mourning brethren, when Martin hurries up to them with tears and lamentations. But then, laying hold, as it were, of the Holy Spirit, with the whole powers of his mind he orders the others to quit the cell in which the body was lying; and bolting the door, he stretches himself at full length on the dead limbs of the departed brother. Having given himself for some time to earnest prayer, and perceiving by means of the Spirit of God that power was present, he then rose up for a little, and gazing on the countenance of the deceased, he waited without misgiving for the result of his prayer and of the mercy of the Lord. And scarcely had the space of two hours elapsed, when he saw the dead man begin to move a little in all his members, and to tremble with his eyes open for the practice of sight. Then indeed, turning to the Lord with a loud voice and giving thanks, he filled the cell with his ejaculations. Hearing noise, those who had been standing at the door immediately rush inside. And truly a marvellous spectacle met them, for they beheld the man alive whom they formerly left dead. Thus being restored to life, and having immediately obtained baptism, he lived for many years afterwards; and he was the first who offered himself to us both as a subject that had experienced the virtues of Martin, and as a witness to their existence. The same man was wont to relate that, when he left the body, he was brought before the tribunal of the Judge, and being assigned to gloomy regions and vulgar crowds, he received a severe sentence. Then, however, he added, it was suggested by two angels of the Judge that he was the man for whom Martin was praying; and that, on this account, he was ordered to be led back by the same angels, and given up to Martin, and restored to his former life. From this time forward the name of the sainted man became illustrious, so that as being reckoned holy by all, he was also deemed powerful and truly apostolical.

As a result of his privation and religious solitude in Gallinaria, where he had lain himself open completely to the Lord, Martin had become aware of receiving the 'firstfruits of the Spirit';[4] it was a sense of well-being and of rightness that longed to find expression in holy activity. As Antony had taught those who came to him in the desert, what he and his fellow hermits were doing out there was nothing new;

others had been out in the deserts before them and had been taken hold of by the Spirit, had raised the dead to life, penetrated into the secret recesses of the human mind, fought spiritual and physical enemies and spoken with angels. The Christian hermits were but a fresh and lively manifestation of the spirit of prophecy, a new crowd of Elijahs and Elishas, and groups of new 'brotherhoods of the prophets', numbered as befitted the Christian, rather than the old dispensation in hundreds rather than fifties.[5]

Martin also seemed to know all along from childhood that he was preparing for a ministry among the catechumens and the *energoumenoi*, and the growing awareness of the charismatic power within him helped him to recognize that the moment would soon come for him to use it. The moment he heard, on his return, of the death of the catechumen, he sensed that here was another opening round in his battle with Satan. Death was Satan's power over human beings.[6] Christ had brought to nought this power; Martin, full of the Spirit of Christ would demonstrate to Satan that he was beginning to lose his grip.

The moment of death itself is one of the hardest things to define, even with the skills of modern medical diagnosis; and there was ample room for wild miscalculations in the ancient world. In the public library at Poitiers is to be found this quaint example:[7]

> Towards the end of the eighteenth century in Poitiers, the wife of a wealthy goldsmith of the name of Mervache, died. The funeral service was held at the church of St Didier in the centre of the town. A grand ceremony, somewhat pretentious, took place and the lady was buried with all her jewellery and rings and bracelets. This was too much for the sacristan, a certain Nortier. He planned to open the grave and rob the corpse at night. This he proceeded to do which was not difficult, because the earth was freshly dug. He took off the lid of the coffin and started to take all the jewels, which were considerable. There was one ring however, which would not come off, so he took the knife and made an incision in the finger so as to slide it off more easily. Whereupon the lady awoke . . . he fainted . . . and on waking he found her gone. She found her way to her husband, who in his turn fell in a swoon on seeing her return all bloody. The chronicle says that Mme Mervache lived a number of years and that she had three children!

The miracle in the resurrection in Ligugé, however, lay in Martin's authoritative attack on the dismal situation, converting misery to hope. Having obtained solitude, he is silent in prayer till he senses the Spirit taking hold of him. Like Elisha he stretches himself on

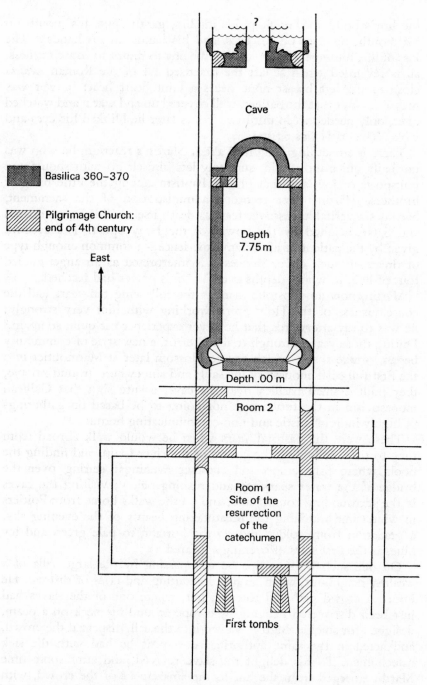

Cave

Depth
7.75 m

Depth .00 m

Room 2

Room 1
Site of the
resurrection
of the
catechumen

First tombs

East

■ Basilica 360–370

▨ Pilgrimage Church:
end of 4th century

9 *Excavations at Ligugé (based on plans in Dom Jean Coquet,* L'Intérêt des
fouilles de Ligugé, *Société des amis du vieux Ligugé, 1968)*

the boy's body and, as Sulpitius implies, gently 'puts his mouth on his mouth, his eyes on his eyes, and his hands on his hands'.[8] The kiss of life, message, prayer, willing the boy to return to consciousness, all is rewarded when at last the practised ear of the Roman *medicus* close to the left breast bone hears a faint heart beat; 'power was present'. After that the patient, well covered up and warm and watched over, only needed sleep until two hours later he blinked his eyes and woke. The crisis was passed.

There is something delightful about Martin's reaction, he who was normally quiet and placid, suddenly lets himself go with shouts and transports of joy, and that private baptism among the little band of brothers, Martin's first recorded administration of the sacrament, becomes a veritable passover feast as death itself had been conquered and Satan insulted by the power of the Holy Spirit. The account given by the patient of his dream experience – a common enough type of dream in such circumstances – is interpreted as an angel-guided tour of hell, to whose depths even Martin's prayer had reached.

Martin, now an apostolic man, in the following ten years had the consciousness of the Holy Spirit working with him very strongly; he was to say afterwards that he never experienced it quite so again.[9] During those years, through trial and error, a new style of community began to take shape, which was to blossom later at Marmoutier into the first full-scale monastery in Gaul; and somewhere around AD 370, they built a small basilica over the cave, a sure sign that Gallican monasticism in the future was not going to be based on gatherings of highly individualistic and non-communicating hermits.[10]

These were the pastoral years when he would walk abroad from time to time, following the course of the river Clain, and finding the pools where fish jumped on summer evenings; staring over the bridge at the water sparkling and rushing below; visiting the caves in the surrounding countryside; and on the walks home from Poitiers in wintertime watching the breathtaking beauty of the evening sky, a gradation from golden red on the horizon to pale green and icy blue, as the first stars of evening appeared.

On one such walk as this he was passing by the large villa of a wealthy neighbour, when he heard shouting and cries of distress. He joined a crowd gathered round a hut, where one of the slaves had just been discovered hanging by a rope around his neck on a beam, designed for suicide. Martin walked into the cell, dispersed the crowd, and acted in the same authoritative way as he had with the sick catechumen. To his delight the slave revived, and after some time Martin emerged from the hut to the amazement of the crowd, with the slave limping along beside him gripping his right hand for support, as he led him slowly up to the porch of the villa.[11]

Two such powerful healings in an age when anything remotely approaching scientific diagnosis was out of the question were enough to put Martin's sanctity beyond all possible doubt, and rightly so, for they were courageously done. In fact as so many hermits were finding at this time and since, there is a magic about dedicated solitude, which seems to fascinate the world, and Martin's name and fame were spread abroad throughout the whole region. Apart from the fact that all he wanted was his solitude here with the brothers, and the calmness of content to be engaged in a struggle the end of which was surely known, he had many things about him that made him a desirable prize for any town looking for a new leader. He was a man full of the Holy Spirit, which had been proved by his raising two people from the dead; he was under the guidance of the hero of Gaul, Bishop Hilary at Poitiers, and he had proved his ability to lead and keep men together in community.

At Tours, a hundred or so kilometres away, in the year AD 371, bishop Litorius died and the clergy and people were looking for a worthy successor. Appointments to bishoprics, since their holders were becoming increasingly prestigious figures, were now of interest to emperors and governors, who were getting into the habit of themselves placing nominees before the local clergy and people, with suitable encouragement and sometimes veiled threats that they should agree to their nominees. The bishops were to meet at Tours on a certain day in the presence of the whole congregation to consider suitably vetted candidates to fill the vacancy; their well-ordered plans were to be rudely upended, and the even tenor of Martin's life shattered.

Martin looked up one day soon after he had restored the hanged slave to life, and saw a large deputation of the people of Tours standing around him. They had come all this way, about a hundred kilometres or so, they said, to invite him to be their bishop. As Martin listened to their excited spokesman Ruricius, explaining the situation, he was filled with revulsion at a prospect that spelled the end of his hard-earned freedom. Watching them as they stood there eyeing him, he knew that their minds were made up; these people had come for him in the same way as the burly recruiting officer and his squad with their chains had come in his childhood to take him away, and to shatter his ideal of solitude and quiet.

He refused to move. Ruricius then told him a fabricated tale of how his wife was ill and pleaded with Martin to come and heal her; as he pleaded he fell down on his knees and begged him to come. It was a signal for the delegates to surround Martin and carry him off protesting on to the road to Tours. Sulpitius uses the same word to describe this abduction as was used to describe the capture of a runaway deserter from the army,[1] and it is a word that implies seizure and manhandling.

Now a captive, Martin had no option but to let them carry him off or to sit on the horse or mule, whose every step took him away from his beloved Ligugé he was never to see again. The first stage of the road between Ligugé and Poitiers was lined with people from Tours, who hailed him as he came, providing him with a kind of guard, the reason for which was fairly obvious, for if the men of Poitiers heard about it in time, they might well turn out in force to prevent this prize being snatched from under their noses.

This extraordinary method of selecting a bishop and the subsequent disorderly consecration of Martin in Tours, demands some explanation. During the four or five decades after the emperor Constantine's accession, the church was not only being swamped by multitudes of new converts it was no longer able to control or instruct properly, but the very structural pattern of its leadership was changing beyond all recognition. The rough and ready action of the people of Tours was among the last protests of those who had lived through the years of the church's triumphs under persecution, before the curtain fell on those times for ever.

The appointment of bishops in primitive times had been a matter of the greatest importance for the healthy development both of the local church community and of the wider community of churches of which it was a part; for everything revolved around the person of the local bishop as the chief pastor of the Christian flock. Clement, bishop of Rome, writing about the year AD 95 in a letter to the Christians of Corinth, points out[2] that the apostles themselves in their lifetimes had appointed bishops and deacons for all the churches they founded, and that after their departure the appointments were made by 'other notable men' (*ellogimon andron*), with the agreement of the whole church.

In the two centuries that followed, when the churches grew rapidly in spite of fierce persecution, this method of appointment, sketchily outlined by Clement, had developed into a common pattern recognizable throughout the Christian world. On the death or removal of its bishop, the whole body of faithful Christians with the presbyters, and deacons, all with the right to vote, would meet to appoint his successor. It was a procedure that flowed naturally out of the concept of the apostolic teaching that the Priesthood of Christ was to be exercised through the company of baptized believers,[3] delegating the particular authority of presidency to a person who had proved himself to their satisfaction to have the qualities and talents necessary for leadership. Then, in order to ensure that their local bishop was acceptable to the wider fellowship of the church, the local congregation had to notify the bishop of the largest city near, the metropolitan, and the neighbouring bishops, so that they could give the seal of their approval, and come on a set day for the final election and consecration of the new bishop, in the presence of the whole body of faithful Christians.

At the time of the emperor Constantine's accession there were thus three groups of people involved in the election of a local bishop, the whole body of worshippers, the clergy, and the neighbouring bishops of whom the Council of Nicaea laid down there must be at least three present;[4] and the active participation of all three groups was essential. It was a remarkable system so long as the local church could be seen as one congregation, however large, for it ensured that the local people who knew their natural leaders, had the right to choose one for their bishop; and it also enabled the metropolitan and his fellow bishops, either to veto anyone who was obviously unsuitable or to make suggestions of others known to them to have outstanding gifts and qualities for leadership in the faith. Indeed, so successful was the system that the very organization it created was seen as a wonder in the ancient world, and this ultimately led to its corruption.

The policy of Constantine and his immediate successors had had an overpowering effect on the church structure for which its members and leaders were not ready. Though Constantine might harangue the bishops at the Council of Nicaea, they were a favoured group in his eyes, above even many of his own magistrates and governors. Having made them financially secure, he loaded them with presents and titles if they favoured his policies, and threatened them, like any other of his political agents, with banishment and deprivation if they displeased him. It was obvious that having obtained control, as he thought, of the leaders of such a closely integrated and homogeneous body through-out his empire, he was greatly interested in their selection and appointment.

As his reign proceeded, he was seen to be exercising a deliberate policy of deposing bishops from their sees and appointing others in their places, though doubtless in most cases he was careful to observe the formal procedures of election. Although it might look outwardly the same as before, when the great assembly of the faithful in the new basilicas cried '*dignus est*' to the candidate put before them, the emperor's threats and the presence of the military outside to keep 'law and order' made everyone realize that times had changed; and some of the nominees of Constantine and his son Constantius were very peculiar and unsavoury characters with few Christian virtues.

The inevitable consequence of Constantine's policy was gradually to remove the voice of the laypeople in the election of their bishops, and this tendency can be traced in the decisions of the various councils that met during the period to deliberate about it. In AD 341 the Council of Antioch stated clearly that there were three parties to the election of a bishop, the metropolitan, the clergy and the people of a diocese or church – all were necessary for a valid election and if any one party disagreed the election was void. In AD 347 the Council of Sardica, cancelled an election made by the 'clamour' of the people, with suspicion of bribery or undue influence. In AD 365 the Council of Laodicaea, assigned the selection of the new bishop to the metro-politan with the concurrence of his neighbouring bishops, and forbade the turning over of the voting rights to the people. Gradually from that time on the vote of the people was, although formally necessary, tacitly ignored until, in the time of the Emperor Justinian, they are referred to as 'the rich or those in high station'.[5]

When the announcement was made that there was to be an election of a new bishop and a date fixed for the gathering of the Metropolitan and other bishops to visit Tours for the purpose on 4 July, the people of Tours were having none of this; they were certainly not going to be left out, and certainly not going to leave it to those who were rich or in high station.

Bishop Litorius had been one of themselves, a man of great piety, elected by the people, and under his leadership the church had grown rapidly; one of the senators of the town had presented the church with a villa and this had been changed into a church during his time. Before that there had been only one other bishop, Gatien, who had been sent to them to found a church in the city, had been rejected by the inhabitants and during the Decian persecution had gone out into the caves outside the city and carried on the Christian work there. That was the kind of church and bishop that the people of Tours wanted, they were not in the frame of mind to accept any imperial nominee who might come in as an unknown official to rule over them and support the imperial taxation policy with its swingeing demands.

Thoroughly to confuse the issue and to make the perfectly legitimate aspirations of the people of Tours even more capable of being expressed vigorously, a further political development had taken place which had considerable bearing on their action. Whilst Martin had been at Ligugé, a number of important events had taken place. The emperor Julian had died after a short and brilliant, if provocative reign, whilst campaigning in Persia in the year AD 363. On his death it was clear that his attempt to restore paganism and the old empire had failed, and his effective successor, the emperor Valentinian I, born and raised on the frontier of Pannonia, turned out to be a simple and almost illiterate, but exceedingly just, orthodox Christian.

He set about restoring the situation as it had been before Julian's reign, the bishops and clergy were restored to their original status with all their privileges and titles, and, most importantly, grants of money, though these were somewhat reduced.[6] He was a strong disciplinarian, personally brave, though often severe and cruel. With regard to Christianity he was tolerant, and was determined that all whose opinions differed should be allowed and encouraged to live together in peace, though his task was somewhat complicated by the fact that his wife Justina was an ardent supporter of the Arian heresy. He was ruthless with all dishonest civil servants and tax collectors, and as a result of his strictness a number received the death penalty.

One of his special concerns was for the welfare of the cities under his jurisdiction, seeing them as centres of intellectual and social development; and from this concern sprang the creation of a quite new rank in the civil service, with the title of defensor.[7]

The defensor was to be a kind of Ombudsman, or protector of the people on behalf of the emperor, his special representative in every city, to whom the highest and the lowest could turn if they felt they were being unjustly treated. The defensor had in theory the right of entry immediately into the emperor's court and the right of a personal audition with him. In order to ensure that the defensor was known to everyone, it was stipulated that he was to be elected at a general meeting of the townsfolk. It was natural that not only the emperor, but the people of the towns and cities should look towards the restored episcopate to find candidates for this high office, which conferred on the bearer the same status as a magistrate, for the bishop had the necessary position within the church to exercise this kind of authority and to summon behind him the goodwill of a large section of the community. The old tradition, cherished from the primitive times of the church, that the election of the bishop should involve the whole community of believers, took a new turn as it became tied up almost unconsciously with the developing ideas of Roman government.

Unfortunately for Martin he exactly fitted the bill of the people of Tours; he was the one man they knew who would lead them back to the spirit of early Christianity, where a bishop was a father in God of his people, and he was the one man whom they could trust to stand up to the emperor face to face, and for no other reason than that he wished to see Christ's ways observed in public life. And then, deep down, under all the veneer of Roman civilization they were Celts. Theirs was a culture built around the secret religion of the Druids, from whom it was an honour to be descended,[8] and Martin, though a completely dedicated Christian, possessed many of the Druid's characteristics, with his strange way of living in a cave in a wooded valley, and his mysterious charisma.

So as they approached the city their excitement knew no bounds; people came out and lined the roads, and as they marched triumphantly along they cried as if getting practice for the election day *'Dignus est'* – 'happy the Church with such a priest!' Their victim, however, sat among them passively, displaying that most highly prized of all the virtues of old Rome, the Stoic virtue of patience. Being a man of few words it must be left to the more articulate Augustine to sum up the feelings of what it is like to be in such a situation: 'A slave may not contradict his lord. I came to this city to see a friend. . . . I was grabbed. . . . I was made a priest . . . and from there I became your bishop.'[9]

The excited crowd arrived at the small church built by Litorius from the senator's villa, bringing Martin with them on 4 July at the time appointed for the election. The metropolitan and bishops from the neighbouring churches were there, the only one of them named being called Defensor. It could have been the bishop of Arles, who bore that name, or it could have been one of the new defensor-bishops, sent to preside over the election. They had their own short-list of carefully vetted candidates, who certainly bore no resemblance to the people's choice. Martin was pushed forward as was the custom, amid loud shouts of: *'Dignissimus est!'* and *'fortunata est ecclesia Caesarodoni!'*,[10] and they pushed him on until he stood almost like a criminal before the raised throne of the metropolitan bishop, who sat there surrounded by his fellow bishops from the neighbouring towns, behind the holy table.

The bishops and some of the leading men of the city, who, according to the new order of things, felt themselves entirely responsible for making the choice, immediately voiced their objections. It was not seemly that one with such a pale and cadaverous countenance should rule in the church of Tours. The bishop and chief magistrate must be a man of healthy Gallic appetite and able to entertain and be entertained by the nobility and even on occasions the emperor. Then there was the matter of clothing; Martin's was mean to the point of insult and this was a very delicate point. None of the clergy at this period wore distinctive vestments or clerical dress in conducting worship or as they went about their day to day tasks. Pope Celestine (AD 422–32) even wrote a stern letter to the bishops of Gaul some thirty years later, for they were beginning to introduce items of their monastic garments into the robes used for worship: 'we clergy,' he wrote, 'are to be distinguished from the people and from other men by our teaching, not by our vesture, by our lives and not by our dress.'[11] At this period the only people who wore any kind of distinctive religious dress were the ascetics and monks, whose rough garments were beginning to take on the nature of a uniform. Paulinus of Nola describes their unprepossessing appearance in one of his letters to Sulpitius, and in doing so describes Martin as he appeared on this occasion: 'poor fellow servants, pale of face like ourselves – not proud men in embroidered garments, but humble ones in bristly clothes of goats' hair; . . . men draped in rough cloaks, fastened up not with a military belt but with a length of rope.'[12]

A group of upper-middle-class men, who were beginning to understand and bring into some orderly control this exciting new career of bishop, were here faced with one of their number who had kicked over the traces for some obscure religious motives. As he stood there dumbly before them with the weight of the unsought popular vote strongly in evidence behind him, Martin seemed to be telling them that there was more to this new career than they had as yet understood.

The last straw was the haircut. It is extraordinary how a haircut can quickly become a symbol. Sulpitius describes Martin's hairstyle, '*crinem deformem,*' ugly hair; the word that describes the deliberate ugliness of the haircut or tonsure that was to become the hallmark of the Celtic monks. Paulinus describes it in detail:[13]

> men with hair not long and trimmed over a shameless brow, but cut close to the skin in chaste ugliness, half-shorn irregularly, shaved off in front, leaving the brow naked . . . they should be even eager to look disreputable. . . . The appearance, disposition and smell of such monks cause nausea in people . . .

An unique cut, different to the complete baldness of the eastern monks or the neat basin cut of the Romans, it gave an extraordinarily wild appearance and was scathingly nicknamed the tonsure of Simon Magus. That an ex-officer of the imperial guard should debase himself to this extent was too much for this new elite clerical caste determined to maintain a high standard in their profession. So, as they had every right to do, they objected vigorously, '*non dignus*', and gave their reasons. The objections were loudly voiced to the excited crowd by the defensor-bishop whose name certainly gave him authority to call for order, but even as he spoke he was laughed out of court by the whole congregation.

Then an extraordinary thing happened, whether by accident or design will never be known. The presiding bishop felt that the time had come to proceed with the eucharistic service which provided the background to the election and consecration, and ordered that the lessons should be read, perhaps in the hope that the familiar words and actions would restore calm. All waited for the lesson but there was silence.

The reader whose turn it was to read the lesson had been unable to get through the mass of people crowding around the church door, and the lull became an embarrassed silence. One of the deacons snatched up his psalm book to read at random and found himself saying: 'Out of the mouths of babes and sucklings thou hast perfected praise; because of thine enemies, that thou mightest destroy the enemy and the "defensor" ' (vulgate for avenger). The oracle of God had spoken, the Lord himself was in the sentence and a great roar of delighted applause filled the church.

It is impossible not to feel that the oracle was rigged, for something like this happened on other, similar occasions. In these decades of transition in the matter of the appointment of bishops, mob rule, often with excellent results, had taken over and there was a kind of pattern to it. At Milan, three years after Martin's election, Ambrose the much respected governor of Liguria, had gone to the election of the new bishop on the death of Auxentius, to ensure fair play and to see that no bones were broken, for the parties were at loggerheads. A child had suddenly shouted during a moment of silence 'Ambrose for bishop', and, although he was not then even baptized, within seven days he was consecrated and became one of the most illustrious bishops the church has ever known. Augustine, whose feelings have already been described had simply gone to the church at Hippo Regius one Sunday, feeling quite safe, because the bishop himself was conducting the service; but the bishop seeing Augustine standing there, preached a sermon on the desperate need of the church for a learned presbyter and went on to such effect, that the people took the hint, turned round and saw Augustine standing there. They grabbed him and without more ado pushed him up to the bishop's throne for ordination.[14]

The people of Tours took Martin, now their anointed bishop and installed him in the bishop's house which was part of, or near, the church. There were no removal expenses to be met; for he had no luggage and slept on the floor. He continued his life of prayer as if nothing had happened; but it is difficult to believe that he did not hanker that summer evening for the walk along by the river bank at Ligugé and the spot where he knew a large pike lurked.[15]

Part Three

Parish pastor

The people of Tours were to learn very quickly that they had found for themselves a very unusual bishop. For the first months after his appointment Martin lived in the bishop's cell or *secretarium*, which every church possessed – a relic of the days when the church had been but the largest room in the Christian villa, reserved for worship, and with surrounding rooms leading off it.

The *secretarium* was the place where the church's business was conducted under the care of the deacons.[1] It was a mixture of church hall and parish office, used for the meetings of synods and even councils and for the dispensing of Christian justice when the bishop acted with his full powers as magistrate. In larger churches the space was divided up so that there was a room where the bishop could prepare for the services in quiet or go to read, pray or study, away from those who were conducting the affairs of the church next door.

The people and presbyters and deacons of Tours had become used to the idea of their bishop being a man involved in their daily affairs, and the numbers of people seeking private audience with Martin grew until he could stand no more. In contrast his successor 200 years later, Gregory the historian, was a man contented to be constantly in demand; chief executive of a burgeoning church bureaucracy, organizer and administrator, he thrived on it; he disputed with heretics, cared for the church plate, conferred with kings, adjudicated in disputes, built churches, had many properties to administer and numerous servants to govern; he entertained important visitors from all over the Christian world, travelled widely himself, and in between all these duties, wrote books.[2] He was the type of bishop Constantine's establishment had prepared the way for; it was not the kind of bishop Martin was prepared to be.

Everything in him revolted at such a concept of the chief pastor of God's flock; he was determined to rediscover the style of spiritual leadership which, to use John Cassian's phrase, prevailed: 'as long as the primitive church retained its perfection unbroken'.[3] He understood enough about that style of spiritual leadership to know that it did not consist of business and socializing, and so, apparently with no warning, he moved from the bishop's cell, from the church precincts, and from the city altogether. He walked out to the caves that dotted the cliff face on the south bank of the river Loire, a scene similar to, but on rather a grander scale than Ligugé, and having come to a large flat meadow between the river and the cliffs he set about building for himself a small wooden hut immediately at the foot of one of the highest cliff faces. It was to be his home for the rest of his life – Marmoutier.

He came here for no nostalgic reasons; rather it was a symbolic gesture that sprang from the heart of his silence. In these caves in the cliffs St Gatien, the first bishop of Tours, had carried on his ministry, secretly celebrating the eucharist with the first few fellow Christians during the persecutions a hundred and fifty years before. Martin was spelling out clearly that he wished to live as bishop in the spirit of the martyrs and confessors, where the church might have to carry on its work without their bishop, everyone to the humblest Christian child dedicated fully to the dangerous and demanding task of the pastorate and evangelism.

Then again this lonely place in the valley with the wooded cliffs, away from the din and hubbub of the city had a deeper significance of which Martin was perhaps yet barely conscious, but which was to open for him the way into the heart of the Celtic peoples. The old Roman religion was a religion of city and shrine; a religion that had no central shrine in a city where the appropriate rituals before the gods might be performed was incomprehensible to a Roman, and could only imply atheism. Christianity and Druidism therefore, the two religions that seemed to have no fixed shrines, had been banned by the imperial authorities on the charge that they were believed to perform human sacrifice in secret at their assemblies.

Christianity, by its persistence, had won the day and overcome the opposition of the emperors, until its bishops had become embedded in the structure of society; but what had happened to the Druids will never for certain be known. There are indications that they took refuge in Britain, and were driven thence to Ireland, but their departure left a great and deeply religious people without their leaders. The Romans had built shrines everywhere they had gone, and were quite prepared to share them with the local inhabitants and even to combine their gods with theirs, but it was not wholly satisfying to the Celts, whose religion was far more all-embracing and secretive than the perfunctory religion of nods and rituals that satisfied the Romans.

When Christianity had first been introduced to the Celtic leaders that August day in AD 177 in the amphitheatre at Lyons, they had recognized that here was an intensely all-embracing and secretive religion with undertones very similar to their own. When they had watched fascinated as the servant girl Blandina was tossed by the bulls till she died in agonized ecstasy before their eyes, or had stared absorbed at Attalus, the Christian nobleman as he sat roasting on the iron chair, defiantly proclaiming his faith in the other world and Christ its chief – their intense personal courage in such unarmed single combat had struck deep chords.

The Celts were ready for Martin, this new chief priest of the Christian religion in Tours, who had forsaken the central shrine in the city of which he was custodian in favour of the caves and woods and valley of Marmoutier; one who by personal daring had caused two great armies to separate, who had raised two people from the underworld, and who had started to collect around him a band of young men at Ligugé. Pomponius Mela writing somewhere around the year AD 50 had described how the Druids had appeared at the time and added: 'they teach many things to the nobles of Gaul in a course of instruction lasting as long as twenty years, meeting in secret in a cave or in remote woods and valleys.'[4] The scene was set at Marmoutier for a new flowering of Celtic culture under Christian leadership, and the young nobles soon began to make their way there from all over Gaul and Britain.[5]

No sooner had Martin finished building his hut than the crowds began to gather round him again, for it seemed that the charisma of this mild-mannered old army officer, so keen on hours of loneliness with God, had the paradoxical power to attract the very human company he consistently shunned, both young and old. This time, however, they were different crowds than those who flocked to his cell in the city, and he dealt with them in a quite different way. The men and women who came to him now knew he was not there to give them personal comfort, or to conduct the business affairs of the church with them, or to listen to their cases; all that had been delegated to the deacons of the church in the city. Had not their role been devised by the Spirit of God, to free the apostolic leaders from serving tables to give themselves to the ministry of the word and to prayer?[6] In the same way the day to day direction of the spiritual pastorate had been handed over, as it so often had had to be in the days of the persecutions, to the members of the presbyteral team at Tours. Those who now came to him, came for one thing only, to place themselves under the guidance and discipline of a spiritual master, and to be allowed to settle near him and learn from his personal example. Soon there were eighty men of all ages living in the caves or in a kind of shanty town community around his hut, and the women were directed to set up for themselves a house within the safety of the city.

Amongst this large band there were some soldiers like himself, who had left the army to serve Christ, but the majority of them were such as 'are deemed of noble rank', and in this the members of this first large Gallican monastery were quite unlike the majority of the Egyptian hermits who were mostly simple and unlettered men.

Near Martin, one of his early followers, Clarus, a young nobleman who had learnt quickly the ways of spirituality, began to build a hut for himself. He built it large enough to take a number of other young men, who, it seems, he treated as neophytes with himself as their instructor and go-between with Martin. The others hollowed out the cliff face, enlarging caves that were already there, and building new ones for themselves, (many of which are to this day still inhabited by families) until the cliff face was honeycombed.

All wore the simple black stuff tunic of slaves, with a rope round their waist, and, as a special concession to the colder climate of Gaul, a camel hair tunic, which quickly became part of their distinctive dress, and provided obvious links with the great hermits, Elijah and John the Baptist. The food they ate once a day all together, was of the very simplest kind; at first they ate it perhaps squatting around Martin's hut, when the weather was fine, but eventually they met in the common hut which they had made for themselves, and which must have been of considerable size. Unlike Antony and his followers in the Egyptian desert, they did not spend their time making things for sale, and neither did they buy anything, for they seem to have been quite self-sufficient, though there were periods when they were desperately short of funds.[7]

One of their number, Cato the deacon, managed the business affairs of the community.[8] Himself a skilful fisherman, he saw to it that this side of the diet was maintained from the river. There must also have been a supply of the herbs, broccoli and root vegetables that formed the foundation of all monastic diets and which they grew for themselves probably under his direction. It transpires that they had servants for on one occasion they hired one of the local peasants who kept an ox waggon to fetch them wood for the fires, which they kept going on winter days in their huts or caves.[9]

On being accepted as disciples by Martin, they would bring all that they possessed and place it in the common pool under Cato's charge. Recent legislation had allowed the sons of noble families to give their patrimony away in this manner to the church, and clearly these offerings must have provided a good part of the common funds on which they relied. The only other source of supply were the gifts in kind or money from the faithful, on whose charity Martin depended entirely, even when their supplies were exhausted: 'Let the Church both feed and clothe us,' he said 'as long as we do not appear to have provided in any way for our own wants,' and the brethren had to tighten their belts as they watched a splendid gift of a hundred pounds of silver, given in return for healing work done by Martin, gathered up and sent off for the redemption of captives.[10] There was an odd aristocratic attitude about this means of livelihood, quite different from the careful and energetic husbandry of their resources by the Egyptian peasant hermits.

What they had all come for, however, was to learn from Martin the meaning of prayer and contemplation. The day was ordered to that one end, to sustain the individual spiritual struggle being carried on in the various cells and caves, as men, deprived of normal social intercourse, explored this new world of the mind and sought to pierce through their tortuous imaginings and the battle with Satan and his minions, to find communion with the living Christ, and to hold converse with his saints and angels.

From time to time Martin would hold open dialogue with them all, and they would meet in the common room for prayer perhaps once each day, but certainly on Saturday in preparation for the Sunday worship. They performed no art work, only allowing some of the younger men to transcribe copies of the scriptures for individual monks to use in their devotions. The hours of the day passed thus, alternating between quiet waiting upon God in contemplation, reading passages of the scriptures, and, as light relief, gardening or fishing.

The life of the community was harsh, and as has already been suggested it is not difficult to trace under the pattern of discipline that emerges the source whence much of Martin's ability to hold together and train such a large and mixed company came; for the key notes of Roman army discipline, obedience, poverty and chastity, though not formally enunciated, appear on every page of Sulpitius's account of Marmoutier.

A soldier once came to join the community, having, like Martin, renounced his military career; he had also forsaken his wife by their common consent, and Martin had placed her in the house he had founded for religious virgins in the city. The soldier built his hut away from the rest so as to show that his zeal to follow the hermit's life was absolute. After some time he begged an interview with Martin and rather pathetically asked permission to seek out his wife's company again. 'He was a soldier of Christ,' he said, 'and Martin should allow to serve as soldiers together, people who were saints, and who, in virtue of their faith, totally ignored the question of sex.' Martin exclaimed: 'Tell me if you have ever stood in the line of battle and been present in war.' 'Frequently,' replied the soldier, 'I have often stood in the line of battle and been present in war.' 'Did you ever see any woman standing there, or fighting?' said Martin, and the poor soldier sat confused and ashamed. Martin went on: 'this would render an army ridiculous, if a female crowd is mixed with the regiments of men.'[11] In this exchange Martin is clearly relying on the iron obedience and discipline of the Roman legions rather than any gospel precepts, as he works out the principles on which his monastery works.

It is a reminder too of the ancient rule of celibacy for serving soldiers. The soldier hermit is taught brusquely that even if the rules of the modern army have become so slack that soldiers may contract legitimate civil marriages, it won't do for a soldier of Christ, for whom marriage must always remain a distraction. Having come to terms with his own sexuality, through the harsh conditions of military service and his own spiritual mortifications, Martin was harsh in nipping in the bud any incipient sexuality within the community; it wasn't so much that it was wrong, it was simply inappropriate.

A young monk sat one day before a fire in his cell, with his legs outstretched and wide apart; his cloak pulled back, he was warming his private parts. Martin, with a sensitivity not unlike that of William Blake,[12] suddenly cried out: 'who, by exposing himself is dishonouring our habitation?', and the young man ran stunned with surprise to confess his shame to his neighbours.[13] Martin knew in such a highly charged emotional atmosphere that such self-indulgence could quickly lead to disintegration of morale; though no doubt he might well have counselled the young man as the abbot Apollo did in Egypt to another young man in similar circumstances:[14]

> Think it no strange thing, my son, nor despair of thyself. For I myself, at my age and in this way of life, am sorely harried by just such thoughts as these. Wherefore be not found wanting in this kind of testing, where the remedy is not so much in man's anxious thought as in God's compassion. To-day at least grant me what I ask of thee, and go back to thy cell.

'No soldier on active service entangles himself in the affairs of this life',[15] should have been written over the gate at Marmoutier. Inside this enclosure the conditions of army life on active service were carried to the extreme; it was not a case of low wages, but of no wages at all; it was not a case of handing in all property to the keeper of the legion's chest on arrival at a posting, knowing that every item was checked for eventual return, but rather a free handing over of all possessions never to see them again; it was not a case of demanding the personal wheat ration every week, but of being prepared to go without any rations at all from time to time when there was no money; in short, it was a life of dedicated poverty.

The question could well be asked how it was that with such a totally dedicated community, withdrawn from the world, Martin and many members of his community could come to be recognized as the most powerful spiritual influence in Gaul at this time, exercising a thoroughgoing and painstaking pastorate far and wide. For Sulpitius relates how 'we have seen numbers of Martin's noble young fellow hermits made bishops', and he cannot refrain from adding piously: 'for what city or Church would there be that would not desire to have its priests from among those in the monastery of Martin?'[16] The answer lay in the remarkable sensitivity Martin showed in the delegation of authority within the shared ministry:[17]

> He displayed such marvellous patience in the endurance of injuries, that even when he was chief priest, he allowed himself to be wronged by the lowest clerics with impunity, nor did he either remove them from the office on account of such conduct, or, as far as in him lay, repel them from a place in his affection.

He not only knew how to delegate, but also how to establish and maintain contact and interest with those carrying out the work.

One of the most remarkably vivid eye-witness accounts taken down by Sulpitius describes this quality well, and was witnessed by the Gaul, who had just then left university and joined Martin's entourage.[18] On his first Sunday at Marmoutier the whole community set out with the bishop to walk to church at Tours. A beggar walked along beside Martin and sought a gift of warm clothing to cover his nakedness as it was winter.

Martin, without hesitating, ordered the chief deacon to see that the man was clothed immediately. The party went on up into the church and took their places, whilst Martin, who was to preside over the liturgy, went into the bishop's cell in the *secretarium* and seating himself on his small three-legged stool was soon absorbed in contemplation. This three-legged stool was as important a symbol for Martin as the spinning wheel was to the Mahatma Gandhi. If ever Martin needed to sit in private or public he would use a small milking stool, such as might be found in any cowshed in Gaul, so as to identify himself with the poorest peasants. It was a quite deliberate rejection of the bishop's throne in the new basilicas, where the bishop/defensor/magistrate sat in all his glory in the congregation; for Martin refused such dignity, to emphasize not only his compassion for and sense of identity with the poorest of the poor, but to recall the Christian people to the humility and meekness inherent in the bishop's office as servant, which they would have seen in the caves with St Gatien. The only concession he would make to people's feelings was to cover himself, possibly with a white robe, to hide his rough untended slave's tunic, for the celebration of the eucharist.

Outside in the other room of the *secretarium*, the presbyters and deacons were engaged in conversation and affairs of business, when suddenly the persistent beggar rushed into the bishop's private room where he sat deep in meditation. He complained to Martin that he had been ignored and was frozen to the marrow. Martin immediately turned his back on the man and without removing his cloak, secretly took off his warm slave's tunic and gave it to the man, ready warmed by his own flesh; whereupon the man went out rejoicing. Martin meanwhile returned into his silence sitting on his three-legged stool, naked under his cloak.

When the chief deacon appeared to tell Martin that all was ready and that it was time for him to come to begin the liturgy, Martin replied that he could not begin the service until the poor man was clothed. The deacon pointed out that the poor man had disappeared. 'Let the garment which has been got ready for the poor man be brought in here to me,' insisted Martin, 'the poor man is waiting for it.'

The deacon then, annoyed at the delay and at Martin's persistence, ran out with bad grace to the nearest shop and bought the cheapest and shortest tunic he could find. By the time he returned he was in a towering rage and threw the garment at the bishop's feet. It took him a long while to work out where the garment disappeared to and why the bishop asked him to go out and shut the door behind him; but in the end he understood.

Without a word of criticism spoken, the pompous chief deacon of Tours is drawn to share in Martin's ministry of compassion. He and his bishop were in the future to work as one; for though he might be physically absent for much of the time from Martin, yet the depth of the solitude with God which he had so rudely interrupted was to form a kind of permanent background atmosphere in which the nature and quality of his own work would be constantly tried and encouraged.

The problems and intricacies of church organization gave Martin no pleasure and were only of interest to him when they failed lamentably, as here, to fulfil their prime objective of ministering with compassion. His long hours of silent prayer and brooding over the scriptures had taught him that the heart of Christ's religion is compassionate concern for human need, and, like Christ himself, his longing to help the sick, the poor and the deranged whenever they approached him had been intensified in silence.

He was being prepared for a strange and eventful ministry that was to carry him far and wide over Europe on endless marches and travels, a ministry that finds an echo in modern times in the life of the Mahatma Gandhi. He had started it well in the *ashram* or commune at Marmoutier but:[19]

> he was never the prisoner of his ashram. It was his home, and he would wander across India and return to it at leisure. He was continually being invited to make speeches, to open schools, and to attend conferences. Often he would make the same speech: calling upon his audience to live virtuously and to practise heroism. Sometimes, when praises were heaped upon him, he would rebel, and say that it would be better if public figures felt they were in greater danger of being stoned to death than of being praised. Sometimes too he would find himself thinking aloud about the unknown future, the strange destiny which he knew was reserved for him.
>
> One day in Bangalore, after the students had drawn his carriage through the streets and he had been welcomed like a conqueror, he said very simply and poetically: 'See me please in the nakedness of my working, and in my limitations, you will then know me. I have to tread on most delicate ground, and my path is destined to be through jungles and temples.'

IO

At Marmoutier today as you enter the monastery gates you find yourself in the grounds of a large girls' school run by a group of religious sisters. On request their oldest member comes and conducts you, a large bunch of keys in her hand, on a long winding ascent up the stairs of the cliff face, and admits you to the caves. She then leaves you to wander by yourself into the kitchen garden of the school, where, amongst neatly ranged heaps of manure, some hens peck.

There, by a tall pine tree, is the site of St Martin's cell, nestling under the highest cliff face, to which a spinney of trees clings desperately. To get up into the chapel on the site where his hut once stood, you must walk past the gardener's shed, where Brice, Martin's young successor made his penance, and then climb up a flight of stone steps. At the top you can see laid out below the site of Marmoutier, once dotted everywhere with beehive huts, and the fields and scrubland beyond, leading down to where the Loire flows.

What did Martin do here all day in this narrow cell or in his wooden hut below? How does a person who has chosen the solitary's life occupy his time, having voluntarily deprived himself of all normal social intercourse and any form of entertainment?

Physically not a great deal appears to take place apart from long hours of sitting still, or standing, or lying, apart from occasional breaks for some form of mild exercise. On the other hand it seems that for the right kind of person, granted the solitude he craves, all the creative powers of his imagination are let loose. A modern master of the use of creative imagination, Pablo Picasso, a communist and atheist, has written: 'nothing can be done without loneliness. I have created for myself a loneliness which nobody suspects. It is very difficult nowadays to be alone.'[1] The artist, poet, writer or thinker, left alone to give free rein to his most powerful gift as a human being, creative imagination, finds new worlds begin to open up as he explores the recesses of his mind.

For the religious solitary, however, his withdrawal is undertaken with a view to using his creative imagination for a specific purpose, as one of the teachers of the desert described:[2]

> For this we must seek for solitude, for this we know that we ought to submit to fastings, vigils, toils, bodily naked-ness, reading and all other virtues that through them we may be enabled to prepare our heart and to keep it unharmed by all evil passions and resting on those steps to mount to the perfection of charity.

In his search for the divine charity the solitary seeks to constrain his physical powers by a strictly limited rough vegetable diet, feeding lightly and probably undernourished; he is as a horse fed on hay rather than oats. He will not be beset as much as his well-fed carni-vorous brother, with a Gallic appetite, might be by the grosser urges and the diseases of fullness, and the chances are that he may well outlive him.

His constant reading will be the scriptures, and he will spend hours at this work, not only in study, but in trying to grasp their inner meanings and nuances so that he can identify himself more closely with them. He will read the lives of the saints and martyrs and come to think of them as companions, whose imagined presence in his cell is so strongly felt that he finds himself in actual conversation with them. Unlike his worldly brother he will not take for granted the background of sunshine, stars and the whole world of created things around him, but will meditate, as he sits on summer days outside his hut, on them all as the handiwork of his Creator, and from inside watch the glory of the raindrops hanging on his cell window bars, and glinting in the sun after rain.[3]

For hours he will sit quietly waiting for God to speak to him and at times he will be in a state of great mental confusion as his imagination brings before him strange perversities out of his own heart, and demons who become as really present as the saints and angels, and yet at other times he will experience ecstasy.

He will perhaps break up his day with an hour or two at work in his garden or the communal cabbage patch, and from time to time it will be necessary for him to make a visit to care for a sick brother, or to have his silence broken by a group of disciples, who will call on his wisdom to settle some difficult problem.

Each hermit's week was, however, punctuated by the highlight of the Sunday gathering for the solemn breaking of bread or eucharist. In a quiet and sensitive way the bishops whose parishes had bordered on the Egyptian desert had gradually extended their influence among the hermits and saved them from complete isolation from church life by persuading them, often with great difficulty to choose one of their number for ordination as a presbyter so that they might celebrate the eucharist together each week. In this way the enthusiasm of their spiritual life was passed on to Christians everywhere, and the hermits, in their turn were checked in some of their wildest eccentricities.

This was then the style of interior imaginative life that Martin lived in the cell at Marmoutier, and in which, when he visited him in the later years of his life, Sulpitius found him absorbed. To describe its even tenor, Sulpitius used the image of the blacksmith at his anvil, a description that has added force when it is remembered that among the Celts the blacksmith was one of the most important members of their aristocracy, invested with an almost mystical awe. 'Just as it is the custom of blacksmiths, in the midst of their work, to beat their own anvil as a sort of relief to the labourer, so Martin, even when he appeared to be doing something else was still engaged in prayer.'[4]

Inquisitive, as so many were, about the serenity of this life of prayer, Sulpitius and the Gaul together decided one day to sit outside Martin's cell, in the hope of receiving some spiritual instruction when he came out from his prayer. They waited several hours in complete silence, and then they heard behind the closed door of his hut a confused murmuring that sounded like people talking together. At the same time they experienced a sense of 'divine awe', a condition that lasted for a further two hours.

When Martin finally appeared, Sulpitius plucked up courage and asked him who he had been talking with, and what was the nature of the awe that they felt.[5] Martin, after some hesitation told them: 'Agnes, Thecla and Mary were there with me', and he described their faces and general appearance in much the same way as William Blake described and drew his visitants, and could not understand why others in the room could not see them too.[6]

Agnes, Thecla and Mary[7] were three saints most popular among the primitive Christians and it is intriguing and wholesome that when this old soldier's imagination was let loose in the intimacy of his cell, it fastened on such vivid female company, for they were all full-blooded Christian women, who, in dramatic circumstances, denied themselves the fulfilment of sexual desire in the service of Christ. One of them Thecla, appears even to have been a fictional character, whose author was punished for publishing her rather exotic life,[8] but they were all intensely real to Martin, and so well known that in his imagination they became living companions. In the same way Peter and Paul appeared at times to him, and frequently he received visits from angels.

There is no reason to suppose that these visitants were merely figments of his imagination; human experience is too complex and limited to make any such open and shut judgment, but clearly his imagination with strong visual power was deeply stirred. The 'angels and archangels and all the company of heaven', of his eucharistic prayer was no formal pattern of words; and the conversation that Sulpitius and his fellow listener overheard need be none other than those sometimes uninhibited and vociferous ejaculations that surprise Christians who give themselves imaginatively to silent prayer.

The basis of all his solitary prayer, however, was for Martin the Sunday eucharist through which he had first been drawn to Christianity: in the fringes of it he had served as a catechumen, and in its core he had received his baptism and first communion; out of love for it maybe he had persuaded a presbyter to accompany him to Gallinaria, and on the Sundays of his life he presided over it and the great weekly thanksgiving with a total abandonment of affection in the basilica at Tours. No doubt he offered up his prayers, in the spirit of the primitive church, 'with all his strength' as Justin Martyr had described it being done in the persecuted Church;[9] for the time had not yet come when the liturgical prayers and thanksgivings were a matter of formal words rigidly adhered to.

It is not surprising that members of the great congregation that assembled at Tours saw visions, and that sunlight playing on the incense as he blessed the altar, was a springboard from which imaginations might pierce through the senses and see heavenly fire playing round his head.[10] Something of the intensity of his involvement in this service comes across vividly, when later in his life, he was to be drawn into a concelebration with a number of his fellow bishops, some of whom had become implicated in the murder of those accused of heresy; he was so deeply wounded by the experience that he would never again for the remaining sixteen years of his life, attend a synod, and he felt that spiritual power had been drained from him.

One of the features of the life of prayer that the Eucharist taught him and all his fellow hermits in Egypt, Syria or Gaul, was the power and importance of intercession, as they grew in understanding of the divine charity; for one of the dangers of the hermit's life was absorption in his own spiritual affairs to the exclusion of the desperate cries of fellow human beings for help. Martin, each Sunday was brought face to face with the cries of the people of Tours in their various plights, and especially of the sick and crazy as they were brought to take their place in the church porch.

Dedicated as he was in his solitude to the search for divine charity, he soon became not only one who remembered them in his prayer, but who was prepared to sally forth as their defensor, in fact if not in name, to emperors and governors to plead their cause. One such journey brought him face to face with the very emperor who had created the office of defensor, Valentinian himself.

Valentinian at first refused to see him, but Martin went on hunger strike and sat outside the palace dressed in sackcloth and ashes. In the end he obtained his interview, and the emperor was quite overcome. He loaded him with presents and offers of entertainment all of which Martin flatly refused; for he was determined to retain his poverty and not to be sucked into the retinue of court bishops.

Back in his cell, however, though angels and saints might visit him, Martin knew that before long his imagination would be disturbed often seriously by the visitation of demons and the archfiend himself. It is difficult now to appreciate how everyone from the meanest peasant to the most sophisticated philosopher accepted the presence of demons as a tiresome yet normal part of everyday life, in the ancient world, in the same way as modern people think of harmful bacteria, some of which are controllable, but others rogues that run amok. Every religion in some way or another purported to neutralize or stymie the work of demons. Madness, sickness, incalculable fits of anger or depression, infertility, the waywardness of animals, crops spoilt by pests or mildew, the loud roar of thunder and the flash of lightning, inexplicable economic failure; all these were seen as the work of spiteful or offended gods or demons and if the religious rites did not move them, then either they must have been done badly, or by the wrong kind of person or worse still, the religion itself was not powerful enough and another must be sought.

One of the attractions of Christianity was that in the hands of holy men, especially the hermits, it seemed to work far better than any of the other religions in bringing, for instance, healing from sickness, and even if it did not do away with demons altogether it certainly seemed to hold them firmly in check. The crowd of gods and demons seemed to become more and more complex as every new tribe was subjugated and brought its gods into the pantheon, and to have them all brushed aside in one fell swoop and replaced by two clear-cut categories; God and his angels on the one hand and the Devil or Satan and his demons on the other made life much easier. It helped too to be reassured that God had ultimately the whip hand, and that through the work of His Son Jesus He had already brought Satan and his minions firmly under control. Martin shared this world view with his contemporaries, and his renunciation of Satan brought with it a great confidence.

The concept of the Devil was not for him the dark figure of the god of the underworld with cloven hoof and horns; rather he was an ever-present spirit who could manifest himself either through images built up in the mind, or through people, often quite unconsciously being used by him to torment or confuse. In his dialogue with Sulpitius and the Gaul, after explaining about the presence in his cell of the saints and angels, Martin went on to explain how he was often visited, much to his chagrin, by demons, whom he rebuked by their special names as they came before him. Mercury, he said, he found specially annoying; Jupiter he found stupid and doltish; and another time he explained that Mercury, Jupiter and Minerva were only disguises under which the Devil appeared to him.[11]

Again William Blake, the eighteenth-century artist, poet and seer, provides something of a key to understanding the workings of Martin's mind.[12]

> The connoisseurs and artists who have made objections to
> Mr. B[lake]'s mode of representing spirits with real bodies,
> would do well to consider that the Venus, the Minerva,
> the Jupiter, the Apollo which they admire in Greek statues
> are all of them representations of spiritual existences, of
> Gods immortal to the mortal perishing organ of sight,
> and yet they are embodied and organized in solid marble.

Martin, in his cell, was having recreated in his imagination vivid pictorial images taken from those countless statues that had formed the background of his life since childhood; the streets were full of them, private houses had small versions of them in niches here and there; no stream or pool but there must be one there. They stood silhouetted on the tops of mountains and high hills, and every cross-roads and every village had its shrine with one of them inside. In company with emperors and many perceptive people, Martin knew that the time was fast approaching when there must be a confrontation between the dying culture which the statues represented and the Christianity which had come to replace them. In his hours of spiritual warfare in the silence of his hut Martin was the one being given the clarity of insight to plan the all-out offensive against the images; an offensive that was to lead to their being replaced by the

10 *Minerva*

11 *Mercury (reconstructed from the Colchester figure)*

ancient parish churches of Europe and Britain, the vast majority of which still stand, a solid memorial to his achievements in his cell.

As a result of all this activity a sharp personal encounter with Satan might well have been expected. Its coming shows how as a result of his perseverance in prayer, Martin had learnt the hermit's most difficult art of all – the art of the 'discerning of spirits'.[13]

His first encounter with the Evil One had been near the imperial headquarters at Milan, on his great tramp across Europe to seek the conversion of his parents. At that time he had had, ringing in his ears, bishop Hilary's downright condemnation of Constantius II, the Arianizing emperor – the Anti-Christ, the 'angel of Satan has transformed himself into an angel of light.'[14] Into that phrase was distilled all the concentrated distrust of Christians who held to the ways of the primitive church as against its pampered imperial successor; a phrase that was to remain in Martin's mind through all the experiences in Sabaria, Sirmium and Milan, and on which his imagination was to feed in his cell.

The half-comprehending populace might crowd into the basilicas and gape in awe at the figure of the glorified risen Christ, whose face looked suspiciously like the emperor's – to Martin it was blasphemy; for it was the Devil who had shown Christ all the kingdoms of the world in a moment of time and offered them to him, and here was the emperor of many of the kingdoms of the world taking over the rule of Christ's very kingdom, and masquerading as a Christian.

The full details of what actually happened that day in Martin's cell can never be known, any more than what happened in the desert

near Jordan some 350 years before. At first reading it seems obvious
that it was another of Martin's strong, visual imaginations; but there
is that about it which might suggest it to have been a deliberate hoax,
as about the same time something similar had taken place in Spain,
and the poor bishop there had been deceived.[15] It so happened too
that at the time a young man named Anatolius had joined the group
of young novices who shared a common life with the presbyter
Clarus not far from Martin's hut. Anatolius had set about establishing
himself by various supernatural magickings as one who had superior
spiritual powers, and had had some success; for many young men in
those days had served as acolytes or performers at the more exotic
pagan shrines and learnt some of the tricks that helped the shrines
to pay their way.[16] For him to have scored over the old saint whom
he had already offended, and be able to make a fool of him would
have been quite an achievement.

Be that as it may, as Martin sat in his cell he noticed that someone
had entered and was standing beside him.[17] He looked up and to
his astonishment saw a most glorious regal figure, bathed in light,
and dressed in the imperial robes he had seen so often before; the
purple robe; the golden diadem, wrought with wires of gold and set
with precious stones and pearls, and the jewelled shoes, but above
all and instantly recognizable the tranquil countenance, the fixed
smile of benevolence and the eyes staring into space that were intended
to assure all peoples of the imperial goodwill.

Martin gazed at the apparition for a long time in deep silence,
seeking to discern who it was, and whence he came; from God?
From his own imagining? From the Devil? At last the figure spoke:
'I am Christ; and being just about to descend to earth, I wished first
to manifest myself to thee.' Martin remained silent. The voice spoke
again: 'Martin why do you hesitate to believe, when you see? I am
Christ.' Then at last Martin replied: 'The Lord Jesus did not predict
that he would come clothed in purple, and with a glittering crown
on his head. I will not believe that Christ has come, unless he appears
with that appearance and form in which he suffered, and openly displaying the marks of his wounds upon the cross.' All that remained
of this pantomime figure was a puff of smoke and a disgusting
smell.

From that time on a sense of well-being and assurance took hold
of Martin and remained with him for many years. He had gone into
the silence of that hut at Marmoutier to be alone with God, and to
seek for the divine charity as a gift from Him; in there he had learnt
a great deal about himself and his imaginings; he had learnt how to
control his appetites; he had learnt at first hand something of the
providence of God revealed in clouds and raindrops; he had learnt

how to speak with angels and saints, and to build up a rich imaginative life; he had learnt the meaning of interceding for others before God, and where that could carry him; and finally he had come to grips with the Devil and his minions.

The long creative silences paved the way for his ministry and they were never to be abandoned. He was confident that he had trounced Satan in his cell, alone and unarmed save for the spiritual armour of a soldier of Christ, but he knew that he was waiting for further rounds in more entrenched positions and that he must go out and 'knock him for six'. He must dethrone him from his coward's castle in the aching limbs of old people, and handicapped children, in the minds of lunatics and in the terrifying loneliness of the leper; he must chase him from one captured position to the next, until his name would be but a jest on people's lips. Martin was ready now to sally forth to do single combat; the divine compassion that in his salad days had fetched him off his charger to divide his cloak with the beggar at Amiens, now fetched him out of his cell to go out to do battle on his mule much to the great joy of the people of Gaul.

II

One day Martin was leaving a first floor room when he missed his footing, tripped over an uneven tread, and fell headlong down a flight of stairs. Seriously bruised, he was picked up and laid on his bed, where for some time he suffered great pain, until at last he dozed off to sleep.[1] In the night he dreamt that an angel appeared, washed his wounds and applied healing ointment to his bruises; and the next day he woke greatly refreshed. Martin's dreams do much to reveal his inner conflicts and motivations, and this one shows how he had come to see that Christian ministry of both angels and men as specifically one of healing. His prayer and study of the scriptures had taught him that the bishop in the church was above all one committed to the healing of men's minds and bodies.

Elijah and Elisha, the men of the desert, had been healers whose methods he had long been studying, Jesus appeared to him chiefly as the one who performed healing miracles so that the people might know without question that the kingdom of God was come upon them, and the apostolic band saw their work as involving the continuation of his ministry among the sick; for healing the sick was at once a proclamation of the presence of God's kingdom, and at the same time a sign that Satan, the source of all sickness and mental confusion, was challenged and overcome.[2]

In choosing after much deliberation to exercise this role of healer Martin was in effect once more identifying himself with the mind of the primitive church, for then, as the old liturgies as well as contemporary accounts show, the healing work of the whole body of Christians was yet one more facet that made the Christian way of life so appealing to the ancient world.

A young pagan conscript legionary, a peasant's son, twenty-two years of age, was on guard duty in a town on the banks of the Nile in the year AD 314. A serious epidemic was raging in the town and people lay dying, many without any attention, in the streets. As the young man watched the desolate scene, he noticed here and there small groups of people going about and bending over the sick to nurse them. He asked who they were and was told – 'We are Christians'. He left the army as soon as he could to seek baptism to join this anonymous company whose selfless devotion had captivated him. His name was Pachomius and his story is only known because he ultimately became the founder of eastern monasticism; it was the kind of story that could surely have been repeated on numberless occasions.

The world in which the church was operating at this time was remarkably helpless when it came to the practice of medicine and the healing arts. The whole of medical research had been dominated since AD 150 by the philosopher Galen's hypothesis that the real end of all diagnostic medicine was to find out where the soul lay. Was it in the liver or the bowels and so on; for he supposed that once having found its locality, it would be a fairly simple process to treat it. Whilst he and all his followers had a fairly thoroughgoing knowledge of human anatomy, their preconceptions made anything but the simplest forms of 'treatments-that-worked' quite out of the question. Pliny's comment on the Roman medicine of his day,[3] summed up many an intelligent man's attitude: 'Rome has managed 600 years without doctors.'

The most advanced practical system of medicine, which included forms of elementary surgery, was that of the Roman army, with its wealth of practical experience gained on the battlefield.[4] The *medicus* was an important person, as has been seen, in the legion, and the *valetudinaria*, or hospitals, with their fine drainage systems, and neat rows of small wards for the sick to be nursed back to health, were remarkable achievements, but even they relied heavily on the shrine of Aesculapius which occupied the end room and where the patient on arrival must spend the night in the hopes of receiving a dream which would tell him what was wrong with him and how it could be put right.

In such a background of muddle and helplessness, the Christian insistence that the God who had created the universe had sent his son Jesus Christ to conquer the chief demon Satan and his minions, provided for the sick a real step forward out of fear and helplessness. The fact that the members of the church were prepared to back up this insistence by exercising their healing arts without charge to people in all walks of life, was also quite a novel experience.

The healing ministry of the primitive church was essentially a corporate work, undertaken by the members of the whole congregation, sometimes led by the bishop, presbyters and deacons but perhaps more often by the laypeople on their own. The inspirational source of all their healing work was the challenge to the powers of evil which was represented by the celebration of the Paschal feast, where the catechumens supported by the whole Christian body had defied Satan before entering the waters of baptism. All the familiar rites that had accompanied this most successful act of defiance were there to be drawn on in ministering to the sick, and Martin like every other bishop in the primitive church used them often: the laying on of hands with prayer, breathing over the sick person, signing with the sign of the cross, the kiss of peace, the actual administration of communion, fasting, encouragement to make an act of faith; all these were used but more than all, the oil. It was the olive oil that above all symbolized Christ's presence to heal.

Christ himself had sent out his apostles in his name to heal, and they had anointed the sick with oil,[5] the apostle James very clearly directed Christians to use it: 'If one of you is ill, he should send for the elders of the church, and they must anoint him with oil in the name of the Lord and pray over him: the prayer of faith will save the sick man and the Lord will raise him up again.'[6]

Olive oil – the distillation of much fruit ripened in sunshine into a small compass – had always been to Jew and Gentile a symbol of blessing and abundance. The Jews had used it for anointing kings and priests and holy places; and the Romans, especially the wealthy, used it not only to massage themselves after the bath, to stimulate the sense of health and well-being, but also cooked with it and drank its clear golden liquid as a mild tonic.

At every Sunday Eucharist in the primitive Christian church, there came a point where the bishop paused to bless the olive oil to be used for anointing the sick. Apart from the flasks set aside to be used by the clergy in their work during the week, the laypeople were encouraged to place their phials of oil on a wall near the altar for the bishop's blessing. Afterwards they were encouraged to take the oil home to anoint their sick relatives and neighbours with prayer, and if they wished it, they might also bring to them the eucharistic bread so that they might feel completely drawn into the vivifying experience of common worship.

Pope Innocent I (who became pope of Rome four years after Martin's death) said: 'not only have the faithful the right, when sick, to be anointed by the clergy with the "holy oil of chrism", but also the further right to use it for anointing in their own need, or in the need of members of their households.'[7] This homely ministry, often accompanied by communion, brought to their friends and neighbours in sickness by members of the congregation, gave to the sick person a sense of being cared for in a way that no other religion or institution remotely provided in the ancient world.

The very words of a prayer used by the bishop for blessing the oil at the Eucharist is to be found in the sacramentary of pope Adrian dated around AD 790, but in all probability it is handed down from the most primitive Christian times. It speaks of the oil as the symbol of healing, fullness and refreshment, and is the kind of prayer Martin would have fully approved of even if he did not actually use it:[8]

> Send forth, O Lord, we beseech thee, the Holy Spirit, the Paraclete from heaven into this fatness of oil, which thou hast deigned to bring forth out of the green wood for the refreshing of mind and body; and through thy holy benediction may it be for all who anoint with it, taste it, touch it, a safeguard of mind and body, of soul and spirit, for the expulsion of all pains, of every infirmity, of every sickness of mind and body. For with the same thou hast anointed priests, kings, and prophets and martyrs with this thy chrism, perfected by thee, O Lord, blessed, abiding within our bowels in the name of our Lord Jesus Christ.

Sulpitius gives an account of the oil blessed by Martin, according to this custom, and describes even the shape of the jar sent to the service by the governor Avitianus's wife and how her boy carried it carefully home.[9] It is clear from these accounts supported by many other references, that it was the normal practice for ordinary members of the laity to exercise a healing ministry of their own in Christ's name among their friends and neighbours, chiefly through the use of oil. However, if the sickness was stubborn or serious, then in accordance with the teaching of St James they would call for the bishop and the presbyters to come to supervise a solemn anointing in the home; and Martin's ministry is full of descriptions of such occasions.

The sacramentary of pope Adrian helps to fill out the picture. The bishop is to lead a group of presbyters and sympathetic fellow Christians to the sick man's house, and if possible to bring a choir to sing to him. Water is blessed and the sick person is sprinkled with it, a reminder of his security in Christ through baptism, The bishop and presbyters then lay hands on him with prayer saying: 'The Lord said, cast out devils in my name, and lay hands on the sick, and they shall recover.' If he can, the sick man then stands and the bishop anoints him thoroughly with consecrated oil, on the neck and throat, and between the shoulders and the breast, and then more liberally where the pain is worst, and as he does so one of the presbyters prays that no unclean spirit may remain in the man, but that the power of Christ may dwell in him richly. Communion was then given to the sick man, and if he felt in the mood – as one of the old Irish books has it: 'the sick man sings if he can; if not, the priest sings in his person.'[10]

Such was the tradition in which Martin had been nurtured in the church. From his early days as a catechumen he had been involved in the healing ministry and must have used the blessed oil frequently in his work; indeed it was because of his obvious success as a healer that Hilary had successfully persuaded him to become a recognized exorcist; for exorcism and Christian healing were regarded at this time as the same function.

After Martin became their bishop, the people of Tours were soon asking for his ministrations, and out of the many fascinating instances given by Sulpitius, three will suffice to show the general tenor of Martin's pastoral methods.

At the outset of his ministry he was staying at the home of an important man of affairs, Evanthius, when his son was bitten by a snake.[11] Evanthius carried the child in unconscious, his skin was swollen, the veins enlarged and his stomach distended. Martin ran his hands all over the child's body making a diagnosis and searching for the wound; then having found it he placed his finger close to the incision and with the assurance of an old army *medicus*, he squeezed it hard. The astonished company watched the mixture of poison and blood pour out ('like a jet of milk from a goat's teat') and after a while the boy got up, shocked but better.

There is no mention of prayer or the use of oil or any other symbolic gesture. It is an example of practical first aid knowledge that Martin had acquired from his military service and which formed the common sense basis of all his healing work. He knew enough about the workings of the human body to know roughly when moral encouragement and spiritual healing were called for and would be effective, and when not.

The next instance shows how his practical skill in diagnosis helped him to apply the olive oil of spiritual healing with great effect. He had come on a visit to Trèves to seek an interview with the emperor on behalf of the Priscillianists whose lives were at stake for their unorthodox opinions. Martin, with a number of other bishops had assembled in the church in the presence of a large congregation, when an elderly man rushed in and interrupted the service by pleading with Martin to go and heal his daughter. Martin was bewildered and at first refused to go; but then the other bishops prevailed on him, and he moved off followed by a crowd from the congregation.

On his arrival at the house, Martin lay down and prayed in silence. In the hush that followed everyone knew that these silent prostrations, which often accompanied his healings, were so that he might enter into the familiar atmosphere of the silence of his cell. This instinctive act also served to concentrate the attention of all those who were present on the prayer for healing that was to follow – this was not magic, it was the prayer of faith.

Martin then looked carefully at the child. She had been totally paralysed for a long time and seemed almost lifeless. After a while he asked for oil to be brought, and when he had blessed it with prayer, he poured some of it into her mouth. The child immediately spoke and Martin knew that he had been able to establish a bond of communication with her. Then, as the custom was, he took the oil and started to massage her limbs with it, for it was in them that the disease was at its worst. It is possible even to enter his thoughts as he did so, saying the formula of the exorcist, *memoriter*:[12]

> 'I anoint thee with holy oil in the name of the Father and
> of the Son and of the Holy Ghost, that no unclean spirit may
> lie hid in thee, or in thy members, or in thy marrows, or
> in any joint of thy limbs, but that the power of Christ
> most high and of the Holy Ghost may dwell in thee.'

'One by one her limbs began to recover life till at last, in the presence of the people, she arose with firm steps.' The child was restored to health by a mixture of practical medicine, physiotherapy and psychological insight, all held together and directed by a simple faith that he was being used as an 'instrument through whom the Lord should make a display of his power', and gathering up as it went along all the dynamic power of expectation of those in the crowd who were joining in prayer with him.

Martin's special healing ministry, however, is best demonstrated in the account of his regular visits to the *energoumenoi*, or mentally deranged, whom he blessed on Sundays in the course of the first part of the liturgy and who, during the weekdays were welcomed into the church building under the watchful eyes of the ordained exorcists. Of all the experiments of the primitive Christian congregations to give expression to their new found compassion, their treatment of the mentally sick is perhaps the freshest and most enlightened; it was destined to provide the first halting steps ever towards methodical treatment of the mentally sick.

In the ancient world those who were deemed to be possessed by demons, or as we should say the mentally sick or subnormal, were treated callously and sometimes with excessive cruelty. No treatment was considered possible apart from religious rituals and incantations, where the offices of a miracle worker could be afforded; and, if this failed, the sick person was left to wander about and fend for himself by seeking alms, and if he became a danger to the public was put in chains or into prison; though it had been found that a blow on the head with a hammer sometimes helped.

By contrast the universal custom of the primitive church was to welcome the mentally sick and the handicapped to their services;

for had not Christ himself welcomed them into his company and as often as not had dialogue with them in his teaching It has already been pointed out how they were welcomed into the church porch, where they were watched over during the services by the deacons and exorcists. Many early Christian writers describe their grotesque appearance in the congregations:[13] 'squalid, foul, with hair dishevelled and in rags'; 'marked out by the church as special objects of pity and of special prayer'; 'with them as fellow sufferers might be found the lepers'; and so on.

The church's care for them did not end, however, with welcoming them to share in the services, for during the weekdays they were welcomed into the church building as if that were their home, and were visited there by the exorcists and deacons who laid hands on them with prayer and provided them with food. They were given occupational therapy, such as sweeping the floor of the church, or lighting the lamps, and if they were capable of understanding, they were prepared for baptism.

Martin's regular and unsolicited visits to the *energoumenoi*, who spent their time in the church at Tours, were a sign of his genuine identification with the church of the apostles and martyrs; for it is easy to see that career bishops would not have either the time or the inclination to waste their energies on such trivialities. If they were forced to, as Sulpitius says, they would use 'a multitude of expressions . . . rolled forth' and keep their distance.[14] Not so with Martin. When he left his cell to set out on the four kilometre walk to Tours it was as if they sensed his coming, for perhaps it was a regular weekly visit that they were used to. Some would rush through the building, roaring, some would sit trembling, as if they were awaiting trial by some fearsome judge; and some would take up absurd attitudes, dangling from pegs or projecting stones in the walls. When Martin eventually arrived, he ordered the exorcists to leave the church and to bolt the doors, leaving him in there alone with them.

He was quite clear as to what he was about; he was in individual combat with Satan over these poor creatures. He was carrying the battle from the quietness of his cell to this place where the Lord of Confusion seemed in total command. Clothed in sackcloth and sprinkled with ashes, he lay full length on the floor, and whilst the hubbub and demonic movement went on all around him, he entered into his own silence, seeking communion with Christ.

Then it seemed all hell was let loose; some stood on their heads, others yelled as if in pain; others sat muttering that they were Jupiter or Mercury, and the whole scene was as if the Lord of the Flies himself were determined to retain his grip on these pathetic figures.

For obvious reasons Martin did not attempt to make use in that disturbed situation of any of the symbolic rituals of healing and exorcism, and it is nowhere recorded that any of the sad patients were healed. All that could be said was that the pastor himself cared not only for them, but for the courageous exorcists, the forerunners of the modern mental nurses, to whom the care of the *energoumenoi* had been delegated, and wished to share with them something of the burden they carried.

Martin's primitive-style ministry to the sick, in which the people of Tours and elsewhere shared, marked the end of an era. So far as can be seen, Sulpitius' *Life of St Martin* is the only account that remains of the life of a parish and its bishop from an eye-witness in patristic times. References in sermons, letters and polemics, however, verify that the picture is a correct one. Up to this period healing formed a large part of the day to day pastorate of clerics and laypeople, and provided one of the chief means whereby people were drawn to baptism, for many longed to share in the free health service that the church provided; and so long as the bishops, clergy and laypeople were seen as part of one common enterprise, the healing ministry remained a viable and integral part of the local church activity. But drastic changes were in store.

Step by step the bishop was removed from his people; he was too busy about church affairs to spend time lying on the floor amongst the church idiots, or to go to people's homes to anoint them when they were sick. He might be a very holy and good man, but his role was no longer that of pastor, except in name. In some districts he had become a magistrate and his presbyters became his assistant legal officers; in other districts he was away most of the time at court; and in others he was immersed in the care and maintenance of the ever-increasing amount of church property. By the ninth century, the right to anoint the sick and take them communion had become reserved to the local parish priest, who once a year must go to the bishop at his cathedral to fetch the oil from the Maundy Thursday service. By the twelfth century the anointing, by now a very formal affair with the priest dipping his thumb into the oil and marking the patient with the cross, was reserved only for those about to die, and the service of exorcism had become a specialized rite of 'bell, book and candle' for laying ghosts and frightening witches.

The demented wandered about again as before, untended, and fended for themselves, unless they were a danger to the public when they were chained or placed in prison. A vision had faded and a glory had departed.

12

The bishop of Tours shinned quickly up a ladder on to the roof of a pagan priest's house that was semi-detached to a famous temple. For the moment his role of bishop was forgotten in the excitement of fighting the flames. Amid the uproar of the cries of those below passing buckets and knocking down walls and partitions to prevent the fire spreading, the bishop could be seen standing on the roof and commanding the flames not to advance any further.[1]

Without a word spoken this dramatic gesture urged on the fire-fighters below to superhuman efforts, and the house was saved; but perhaps the oddest and most spectacular aspect of the whole affair was that the bishop had lit the fire himself.

What was it that had changed the godly and tranquil holy man of the cell at Marmoutier into this violent dervish who destroyed pagan people's property far and wide all over Gaul, and yet was prepared to risk his life to save someone's dwelling house? Some explanation is necessary, for it is not as if the rather dull pagan priests and their country temples were an affront to society, rather the reverse; they were very much part of it, and often exhibited a quiet rural charm in their style of life, as in the well known and widely admired story of Baucis and Philemon, the old couple who found themselves guardians and creators of a shrine, after entertaining Jupiter and Mercury disguised as two rejected travellers.[2]

What makes his galvanic activity in destroying temples more surprising is that up to this time, they had been left severely alone. The Gallic church, like so many churches throughout the empire had been mainly confined to the cities and large towns, as if Christianity had become content to remain an almost exclusively urban religion. In the towns and cities the churches were so settled and prosperous as to be the dominant cultural group, with the result that the worship of pagan shrines had dropped off considerably; but no one until

Martin had thought of taking Christianity out into the villages of the countryside, or worked out what were the implications of doing so.

To understand this apparently Jekyll and Hyde aspect of Martin's character it is necessary to recapitulate and to explore afresh the cultural background in which he was operating; for only then does the reason for his action begin to emerge, and his rapid development into the folk hero of the Gallic people find an explanation.

It is not certain whether Martin himself was born a Celt, though everything about him suggests that he acted like one. Christian historians[3] have made much use of the way in which the Roman world had seemed to have been prepared by providence for the coming of Christ, and the quick dissemination of his gospel. The achievements of speculative thought among the Greeks; the expectation of a Messiah among the Jews; the establishment of the Roman empire with its widespread network of communications and its stability, all combined to create an unique seed bed in which Christianity seemed to gather up almost by instinct many of the cultural drives of the ancient world and to absorb and develop them fully. However, the way in which the widespread Celtic culture provided also a preparation for the Christian gospel and also a great enrichment of it is often forgotten.

After their subjugation by Julius Caesar in 55 BC the relationship between the Celtic peoples and Rome had become a congenial one. The Gauls admired the Graeco-Roman culture of their conquerors, their cities, their art, their literature, and their fine buildings, and they greatly respected the well-trained Roman army which, throughout the long campaign in Gaul, had taught them that individual and even tribal displays of dashing bravery ultimately evaporated before well-led and disciplined troops. Roman roads, universities, schools, laws, commerce and improved farming techniques had become a part of the normal background of a Gaul that was preserved in peace by the frontier garrisons; a peace that was evidenced by the continual building of well-planned towns and the large villas that everywhere dotted the countryside. In Martin's time, even though there were ominous signs that the frontiers were weakening, it is true to say that the Gauls had become in many ways more Roman than their conquerors.

When it came to the relationship between their religions, however, there were deep differences. The Romans could never understand the Celts' readiness to hold their religious assemblies in sacred places in the loneliness of the countryside, and with makeshift gods of wood; they were always deeply suspicious of what went on at these gatherings, particularly suspecting them of carrying out human sacrifice – with good reason it seems from the discoveries made in pits near these places of decapitated human heads.[4]

They could not understand the Celts' passionate belief in the afterlife, as a positive and continued existence of the whole human personality; for the Celts believed that the other world was so vividly present all the time that at moments there were no barriers between the two worlds at all. They were completely fearless of death, because they were certain that in the next world they would have fresh bodies, in which they could enjoy more fully all the good and familiar things that were buried with them in their tombs. As the Roman poet Lucan wrote:[5]

> But you assure us no ghosts
> Seek the silent kingdom of Erebus
> Nor the pallid depths of Dis' realm,
> But with a new body the spirit
> Reigns in another world –
> If we understand your hymns –
> Death's half way through a long life.

As for the Druids, the Romans could never quite pin them down, and there were ever strong rumours that they had influenced imperial policy during the reign of Diocletian.[6] It was known that they conducted the sacrifices, gave sentence on those who were to receive the terrible punishment of exclusion from them, and acted as magistrates of the unwritten laws, but they conducted their affairs in secret and therefore were always under the threat of proscription in a very superstitious age. Other, more pleasant, things were known about them, such as that they were practitioners of the healing arts, through charms and practical herbal medicines; and in fact the elder Pliny's famous description of them going in search of the mistletoe describes it as one of their healing medicines. They were supposed too to have power over fire, and the fortunes of battles.

The Romans did all they could to assimilate the religion of the Celts into their own orderly pantheon, but with how much success is not certain. Julius Caesar, with a certain amount of wishful thinking, wrote of the most popular gods of the Celts: 'Mercury was reckoned the greatest of the gods and Apollo, Mars, Jupiter and Minerva were also found as objects of worship', but he confessed he did not speak from intimate knowledge.[7] Much work remains to be done by archaeologists on the sites of the Romano-Celtic stone shrines on hilltops and by wells and streams before a clear picture emerges, but it seems highly doubtful that Caesar's statement meant more than that, having heard the stories of the Roman gods, the Celts listed them according to their immediate preferences.

Just as today many people find it quite possible to join in fully in formal public worship in the conventional churches, whilst at the same time being ardent supporters of other cults that meet secretly, as the Masons, Order of Druids, of Buffaloes etc., so the Celts, whilst paying more than just lip-service to the Roman shrines, must have continued their ways of worship secretly and undisturbed by their conquerors. Whilst it would have been unthinkable for one of the Druids to be asked to officiate at a Romano-Gallic shrine, by Martin's time they had come to be known as highly respected members of society.[8]

When Martin arrived at Marmoutier in AD 370, he came to live among a people whose culture had prepared them to be led, by someone with a powerful enough personality, into the same Christian religion that their Roman conquerors were busily embracing. Martin was exactly the right person, who had arrived at exactly the right place at exactly the right time. He had all the necessary qualifications: peacemaker, fire-chief, ardent believer in the afterlife, dweller among caves and wooded valleys, where he was content to practise his religion without a shrine; teacher of the young nobility; effective and proven master of the healing arts; hater of the Roman gods; authoritative rebuker of the emperor and his governors, but above all the possessor of the *'esprit Gaulois'*, the puissance and dash of individual bravery, ready to challenge spiritual and physical enemies in single combat and always, marvellous to relate, unarmed.

Side by side with the underground development of the spirituality of the Celtic peoples towards Christianity, during the same period, the Romans themselves had been suffering a sea change as far as their religion was concerned, and the story of their failure to uphold their old pagan religion by force in the face of the ever-increasing growth of Christianity has already been told.

On coming to the throne, Constantine had started quietly enough to introduce the Roman peoples to the new religion that had conquered them without violence. At the edict of Milan in AD 313 he and his reluctant colleague, Licinius, had stated that they had begun by[9]

> granting to the Christians and to everyone else the perfect liberty to follow the religion which he prefers, in order that whatsoever Divinity there be in the celestial mansions may be favourable and propitious to us. . . . We have made this rule in order that no dignity and no religion should be diminished.

In spite of this *bonhomie* everyone understood which religion the emperor preferred, and moreover the one he wished his subjects to prefer as well. The pagans and adherents of the eastern mystery religions soon began to detect an ominous note creeping in:[10]

> As to those who hold themselves aloof from us, let them keep their lying temples, if they wish. . . . There are some,

it is said, who pretend that the use of temples is forbidden them. . . . Such would have been my wish; but, to the detriment of the public welfare, this lamentable error still resists too strongly in certain persons.

Constantine died leaving it like that.

His successors maintained and elaborated his policy with laws that were increasingly pejorative towards the practice of heathen worship, and the Arian emperor Constantius II went so far as casually to remove the statue of Victory erected by Augustus, to the great disgust of the senators, who had nodded to it on their way in and out of the senate house. Paganism had had its day, and the young emperor Gratian, beloved of the Gauls, protégé of bishop Ambrose of Milan, and a devout catholic Christian, gave it the virtual *coup de grâce* when he came to the throne in AD 375. He refused to accept the title, which every emperor before him had borne, of Pontifex Maximus, high priest of the ancient Roman religion of the gods, and he ordered the final removal of the statue of Victory from the senate house where it had been restored by Julian. In AD 379, he withdrew the edict of toleration of paganism and implied that the worship of all heathen sanctuaries must cease.

In the year AD 391, six years before Martin's death, Gratian's successor, the emperor Theodosius, after a fierce confrontation with the forces of the old paganism led by an imperial adventurer, Eugenius, at the battle of the river Frigidus, established the laws against paganism that Constantine had wanted to introduce but had not had the opportunity. He issued edicts: 'forbidding sacrifice to idols or people even to enter the temples', and the following years the law was repeated at Constantinople, this time on the penalty of death for infringement.[11]

The scenes that followed on the promulgation of these triumphalist laws for the Christians, were, in the East certainly, most unseemly and the pathetic appeal of the pagan senator to the emperor describes but half: 'these black clothed ones (the monks) run around the sanctuaries with cudgels, stones, bars of iron, and the like, and even with their hands and feet. . . . roofs are broken, walls knocked down, statues broken, altars overturned.'[12] He might have been describing Martin and his fellow monks.

As Martin had sat all day in his cells at Ligugé and at Marmoutier listening to the word of God, the deep undertow of these cultural movements in the world outside had made itself felt. In his silent struggle with Satan there, he had heard the continual mutterings of those names, Minerva, Mercury, Jupiter, until they had driven him to distraction. And not only there, but lying face down on the floor of the church he had heard them coming to him over the babel of sounds of the *energoumenoi*. Those names and the images that expressed them were emanations for him of Satan. He had driven Satan in personal combat from his cell; he was attacking him through his healing work; now he must find ways of carrying the battle one stage further.

His heroes of the desert in the scriptures taught him how he was to go about it. Elijah with his own hands had taught the feeble Ahab how to destroy the heathen sacrifice on Carmel; Elisha had sent his disciple to anoint Jehu, the ardent destroyer of temples of the heathen gods, who had thought up the idea of turning one of their shrines into a public lavatory.[13] Jesus himself had foretold the destruction of the seemingly indestructible temple of Herod at Jerusalem, and later in his fury had overturned the tables of the moneychangers. Fury, that was the missing element in his ministry in the imitation of Christ, the *orge theou*, the anger of God, the righteous anger that boils because the fire that creates it is held in check by the hand of God. To provide it, there was that element in Martin that was in every Celt, ready to be sparked off without too much provocation; it drove them to charge naked, spear in hand, at the well-protected and stolid lines of Roman legionaries; and sometimes, lying on the beach, they had been known to get up and run down into the raging sea to do battle with the waves and die absurdly in the attempt.

He was to go out unarmed to do battle with Satan on his own ground, in the shrines; for the shrines must go, piece by piece they must be pulled down, he would harm no person's life or house, but the shrines must go, and in their place must rise strongholds or guard-posts where Christ's soldiers could keep watch to prevent any counter-attack. That the Roman emperors were behind him with their new laws, and that the Gallic people were looking for someone to come to deliver them from their religion, that had somehow lost its way, was to him incidental, but it helped.

How Martin began his mission to Gaul is uncertain, it could have been on one of his visits to the emperor or one of his governors, but as he passed by the same familiar shrines he had seen on his march across Europe, he had matured during his ten years of solitude, and the sight that before had merely irritated him now infuriated him with an anger he felt to be one with the table-turning of Jesus.

As he passed through the village of Levraux he saw a temple which, in spite of everything had been well kept, well endowed and obviously much used.[14] He determined then and there to pull it down. As soon as he made clear his intentions and his reasons, an angry crowd gathered and drove him out of the village, raining blows on him. Satan had won the first round.

Martin retired and stayed in some nearby lodging for three days in his accustomed solitude; clothed in sackcloth and ashes he fasted and prayed that the Lord would intervene. Two rather substantial angels appeared, as if from nowhere, with spears and shields, to 'furnish protection to Martin, lest, while the temple was being destroyed, any one should offer resistance'.

In the language of the time those angels might well be two Roman legionaries sent from a nearby detachment, whose commander had received a report that the bishop of Tours was having trouble in implementing the imperial decrees. Martin returned with them to the village, 'and while the crowd looked on in perfect quiet as he razed the pagan temple even to the foundations, he also reduced all the altars and images to dust.'

Seeing this extraordinary exhibition and listening to the interjected instructions about the faith as the stones were thrown down, the majority, perhaps with one eye on the two soldiers standing and looking on with approval, realized that an end of an era had come for them; and, 'so that they might not be found fighting against the bishop, almost all believed in the Lord Jesus'. As they looked at the pile of scattered stones that was the temple they had shared so long with the Romans, some even may have smiled at this quaint recrudes-cence of their old religion in its strange new guise. It was a round won by Martin over Satan, but that only 'almost all believed', meant it was a victory only on points.

It is appropriate to think of these temple-smashing exploits as rounds in a contest between Martin and Satan with the gloves off, for they had, not only for him, but also for the spectators, all the thrill and gusto of an individual combat with high stakes as, for instance, in the case of the falling Pine Tree. Where this lively encounter took place is not mentioned, but it has been argued well that it was some-where near Autun, the religious centre and melting pot of the Celtic, Roman and Eastern cultures.[15]

Travelling with some fellow hermits from Marmoutier, Martin came upon a village where there stood a very ancient temple, and beside it, what was obviously an object of veneration, a tall, sacred pine tree. Sulpitius' emphatic 'very ancient' of this shrine, would suggest that this was a Celtic shrine to the mother goddess of the earth, which had received the full Roman treatment of having a stone shrine built near it in joint honour to her and the eastern goddess Cybele. The religion of Cybele, the Asiatic goddess, had become one of the most familiar Roman cults, and had indeed some very attractive features, especially the festivals in connection with the new moon in March, with days corresponding to the mourning of Good Friday and the joy of Easter Day.[16] At the same time there were elements in it that showed a very perverted pattern of sexual behaviour, and involved the cruelty of ritual castration. In its ritual in Rome each year, the day of the 'entry of the tree' was of special significance, when the college of tree bearers – the *dendrophones* – carried the sacred pine, decorated with violets and wool, to the Palatine temple, having cut it down with religious honours.

The people collected to welcome this strange band who stood by their temple, and Martin explained to them in his usual way what he intended to do. The people watched fascinated whilst he and his colleagues pulled down the old temple stone by stone, no doubt with the usual accompanying comments and instructions. The people raised no objection, a fact which indicates that they were Celts watching a Roman temple being dismantled, but when Martin strode over to the pine tree with an axe, that was different. Anyone could build up a shrine in a matter of a few days, but a sacred tree, that took years to grow out of the womb of mother earth herself, that was blasphemy. It was perhaps right that their landmark should be sacrificed from time to time in March with full religious honours in the city, even if they were of another religion, but this blatant insult was too much.

When he heard their angry muttering, Martin carefully instructed them 'that there was nothing sacred in the trunk of a tree, and urged them rather to honour God, whom he himself served. He added that there was a moral necessity why that tree should be cut down because it had been dedicated to a demon.' Here was a confrontation with his own people; the Druid of Christ demanding allegiance from them to an entirely new and all-embracing male Trinity.

> Then one of them who was bolder than the others says, 'If you have any trust in your God, who you say you worship, we ourselves will cut down this tree, and be it your part to receive it when falling; for if, as you declare, your Lord is with you, you will escape all injury.' Then Martin, courageously trusting in the Lord, promised that he would do what he had been asked. Upon this, all that crowd of heathen agreed to the condition named; for they held the loss of their tree a small matter, if only they got the enemy of their religion buried beneath its fall.
>
> Accordingly since that pine tree was hanging over in one direction so that there was no doubt to what side it would fall on being cut, Martin, having been bound, is, in accordance with the decision of these pagans, placed in that spot where, as no one doubted, the tree was about to fall. They began therefore to cut down their own tree, with great glee and joyfulness, while there was at some distance a great multitude of wondering spectators.

And now the pine tree began to totter, and to threaten Martin's ruin by falling. The monks at a distance grew pale, and, terrified by the danger ever coming nearer, had lost all hope and confidence, expecting only the death of Martin.

But he, trusting in the Lord, and waiting courageously, when now the falling pine had uttered its expiring crash, while it was now falling, while it was just rushing upon him, simply holding up his hand against it, he put in its way the sign of salvation. Then indeed, after the manner of a spinning top, it swept round to the opposite side, to such a degree that it almost crushed the rustics, who had taken their places there in what was deemed a safe spot.

Then truly, a shout being raised to heaven, the heathen were amazed by the miracle, while the monks wept for joy; and the name of Christ was in common extolled by all. The well known result was that on that day salvation came to that region. For there was hardly one of that immense multitude of heathens who did not express a desire for the imposition of hands, and abandoning his impious errors, made a profession of faith in the Lord Jesus.

Certainly, before, the times of Martin very few, nay, almost none in those regions had received the name of Christ; but through his virtues and example that name has prevailed to such an extent, that now there is no place thereabouts which is not filled either with very crowded churches or monasteries. For wherever he destroyed heathen temples, there he used immediately to build either churches or monasteries.

The final sentences of Sulpitius' lively account throw light on the new world that Martin, and subsequently his many imitators, were opening up in Europe and Britain. The imperial laws demanded that, when temples were no longer used, they should be handed over for secular purposes, theatres, offices, market-places and the like, and in the East it seems that this is what largely happened.

Martin and his followers in the West had other ideas, and his decision to build either churches or monasteries on the sites of demolished temples, and no doubt out of the timber and stone from them, was to have considerable consequences for western culture. These churches and monasteries were not in any sense parish churches founded for the pastoral care of the people, though they naturally came to provide such a service. They were rather, frontier guard posts, manned by groups of hermits who watched over the sites where victories had been won and ensured by their vigils that the enemy did not return.

Martin himself went round them, when they were near enough to Tours, like some general inspecting the forts, and where he found as at Amboise, some thirty kilometres upstream, that the presbyter Marcellus whom he had left in charge of the group of monks, was being somewhat prolix in destroying the local temple opposite his guard post, he took the matter into his own hands with dramatic effects.[17]

There are many other cases cited by Sulpitius of Martin's campaigns, and all this activity as it built up was a distraction, but he still made sure that he had many hours of solitude in the cell at Marmoutier.

There is a saying that 'there is nothing that succeeds like success', and whilst Martin was going from strength to strength in his battle with Satan, he had perhaps not noted how much he had come to rely on the goodwill of those very emperors and their governors whose spirituality as Christians he feared and distrusted because of their immersion in worldly affairs. He was to learn sharply that even avowedly Christian emperors could be dangerous fellow combatants in the Lord's battle: for their motivations were devious, pragmatic and sometimes overtly vicious, however plausible their Christianity may have appeared at first sight.

Another sharp lesson was waiting to be learnt painfully. It might well be thrilling to trounce Satan in single unarmed combat in front of the cheering crowds as the tree screamed, twirled in the wind's eddy and landed far away. It was not for nothing that that wicked spirit had made his first recorded appearance on the human scene as the snake in the grass.

13

This is a sad story that tells of Martin approaching and passing through the dark night of his soul; and the pathos of it is heightened by his experiencing it all in the background of one of the darkest spiritual hours in the history of the Christian church as an institution. Within the short space of seventy years the church, whose triumphant glory had been shown to all the world in the sufferings of its martyrs in the amphitheatres, had taken four fatal steps which were to demean it into becoming the most highly skilled, cruel and bloody persecuting institution the world has ever known. Martin had to watch it all taking place around him; Rome, Saragossa, Bordeaux and Trèves were names that were to make his flesh creep, and though he might cry out as a prophet against it all, and even compromise his integrity in order to save innocent lives, it was no good, his voice cried in a wilderness.

It all started quietly enough, and everyone was very-well-meaning, but the situation quickly developed and seemed to take control of everyone involved.

On 17 November AD 375, Valentinian, the emperor of the West had died and his son Flavius Gratianus, at the age of sixteen, had come to the throne. He had been well groomed. His tutor, whom he greatly admired, had been Ausonius, professor of Rhetoric at Bordeaux, the same teacher who had taught Paulinus of Nola and possibly Sulpitius. Ausonius, himself converted to a mild and domestic form of Christian life had helped Gratian to think his way through the catholic or Nicene faith and to come to embrace it warmly, and in this process Gratian had been helped considerably by Ambrose, the distinguished bishop of Milan, who throughout his reign was to exercise a powerful influence over him.

Gratian came to the imperial throne as the first Augustus who out of conviction saw the whole empire united under the catholic or

Nicene faith. He quickly showed by his actions that he not only wished to see paganism eradicated but that catholic Christianity should be established everywhere in its place.

The Christian bishops were not long in taking advantage of this new support.[1] In Rome pope Damasus, not surprisingly after the bloody nature of his election, had been arraigned in open court for some capital offence; Gratian himself stepped in, tried the case himself and completely exonerated Damasus. Encouraged by this, Damasus decided to call a council at Rome of all his fellow bishops in Italy. When they met, the bishops made an unanimous appeal to Gratian that was to have serious consequences. They appealed to him to back up their decisions with the strong arm of the law; and if they, the bishops, had in solemn council condemned one of their colleagues and removed him from office, and he refused to leave, then the emperor should intervene to see that the sentence was carried out. It was a momentous and quite deliberate decision that introduced a new dimension into theological debate; and the arguments in favour of the new outlook are to be found in the subsequent writings of Augustine, bishop of Hippo, as he worked out the idea of God's discipline in dealing with the affairs of men.[2] From then on appeals were made by synods of bishops or even individuals, seeking for imperial rescripts to eject recalcitrant bishops from their seats in the cause of law and order.

There were many who objected violently to this new development, with ample justification, and Martin was one. Almost unconsciously he had found himself leaning on the imperial power for support in his missionary labours; now he found himself on a collision course, not only with the emperor but with the majority of his fellow bishops, who were already seeking the imperial assistance in stamping out a new heresy called, after the name of its leader, Priscillianism. The whole situation was all the more complicated because the heretics held views that seemed very similar to those of Martin himself, and Jerome, and Paulinus and the ascetics generally; and the heretics were inclined to overplay their hand as people very well might who went in fear of the death penalty if they should fail to make out their case properly.

Priscillian was a very wealthy man of noble birth who lived in Spain; he was[3]

> bold, restless, eloquent, learned through much reading, very ready at debate and discussion – in fact, altogether a happy man, if he had not ruined an excellent intellect by wicked studies. Undoubtedly, there were to be seen in him many admirable qualities both of mind and body. He was

able to spend much time in watchfulness, and to endure both
hunger and thirst; he had little desire for amassing wealth,
and he was most economical in the use of it.

His studies had led him to take his Christian faith seriously, and
in pursuit of divine truth he had come under the influence of Egyptian
teachers, one Mark, and his two close disciples, the noblewoman
Agapé and Helpidius, a rhetorician.

Their main teaching seems to have been that the practice of rigid
asceticism was necessary in order to prepare the individual soul
for mystical union with Christ. Like monks they were to be recognized
by their pallid features and gaunt appearance, and to add to their
similarity to the ascetics, they taught that sexual continence was
imperative for all Christians, even to the point of denying that marriage
was a lawful state. They were insistent that they taught the catholic
faith of Nicaea, and encouraged all their converts to join with the
bishop at the Sunday Eucharist, though they for some reason did not
consume the wine at the altar when it was proferred to them.

Priscillian was caught up by their enthusiasm and devotion and
joined them in their house-meetings or where they met secretly in
caves. He soon became their recognized spokesman and a large
following began to build up around him, especially of the nobility;
and 'women flocked to him in crowds' attracted by his eloquence,
learning and ascetic features. No doubt also the excitement of the
night vigils helped, when he prayed 'in a state of nudity', but modern
Christian yoga devotees might be offended to have this pleasant
custom brought up against them as reason for the death penalty.
The enthusiastic support of these house-meetings in small groups,
allied with the practice of spiritual rigorism, is some sort of indication
of the sense of loss being experienced by devout Christians in the
formalized Christian life being offered to them then by the state church.

By the year AD 380, so powerful was Priscillian's influence becoming
that two bishops, Instantius and Salvianus, promised him their support.
As soon as this was reported to the metropolitan, Ydacius, it was
decided that a council of bishops should be held at Saragossa at which
Priscillian and the two bishops should be invited to explain their
beliefs and be questioned.

They never appeared, and in their absence the council condemned
them in general terms for the extravagance of their teaching. At
the council the keenest opponent of the Priscillianists was the bishop
of Ossonba, Ithacius, who was to have a very large part to play in
what followed: he was 'worldly, luxurious, shameless, addicted to
the pleasures of the table, just the kind of person to be obnoxious
to holy people'.[4] When the council ended, he claimed to have been

commissioned to publicize the facts about Priscillian's condemnation; and as a result of his labours, being a court bishop, he was able to obtain an imperial rescript from the emperor Gratian himself, decreeing that Priscillian and all his followers 'might be expelled from the cities'.

Such gross and insensitive behaviour provoked a popular reaction. The city of Avila was without a bishop at the time, so Instantius and Salvianus, joined by two other bishops, proposed Priscillian for election; the proposal was quickly taken up by the people and Priscillian was duly consecrated bishop of Avila. Priscillian, now a bishop in the catholic church, with commendable courage decided to make the journey to Rome to put his case before pope Damasus and the church there, that his name might be cleared. He planned also to visit Milan to seek bishop Ambrose's advice and encouragement, knowing him to be a keen supporter of the ascetic movement, and also to have the ear of the emperor.

The little party travelled across Gaul and were much applauded in many places, though they were refused admission at Bordeaux. Here, however, they were welcomed into a large country villa outside the city, by Euchrotia, a lady of great wealth and the widow of a rhetorician. They stayed here for some time at her house and converted both her and her daughter Procula to their way of life, besides many others.

On their arrival in Rome, the little band now swollen in size to twelve, including both Euchrotia and Procula, sought audience with pope Damasus, who had been forewarned of their coming in no uncertain terms by the Metropolitan Ydacius. Damasus refused to admit them, and to add to their frustration and disappointment bishop Salvianus fell ill and died. They moved on to Milan where bishop Ambrose in the same way refused to admit them, and they felt that the cold hand of the official church had gone out against them. When the official church leaders closed ranks like this it boded ill for speculative theology in the church of the future.

Priscillian, a man of spirit, went straight to Verona with his party, where the emperor was in residence, 160 kilometres away. There, with great skill (some accused him of bribery), Priscillian obtained through a friend in court a further rescript from the emperor Gratian under which the three bishops and their supporters were to be restored to their churches and all previous censures against them were to be lifted.

Armed with this document they returned home triumphantly to their dioceses, and, not prepared to leave things well alone, issued a writ against bishop Ithacius on the grounds that he had falsely accused and defamed them. The local proconsul was on their side and bishop Ithacius, realizing that he was now hoist with his own petard and that his life was in danger, fled to Gaul; he made his way to where he knew he was safest, among the court bishops at Trèves, where he had allies and he knew how to use his influence. Whilst he was there licking his wounds, suddenly the whole city was in a ferment of excitement and uncertainty; for news started to come in that the troops in Britain were in revolt, had set up one of their generals, who bore the imposing name of Magnus Maximus a Spaniard, as emperor, and were marching against the emperor Gratian. Gratian fled, and, deserted by his army, was shamefully murdered in Lyons by the master of the imperial cavalry.

Magnus Maximus made his triumphal entry into Trèves in the year AD 383, and as bishop Ithacius watched the procession passing and caught his first glimpse of his new master, he must have been in a state of great uncertainty. He need not have worried, for Maximus was a very ordinary soldier, in the mainstream of the tradition of Constantine as regards the church establishment, and personally devout;[5]

> a man worthy of being extolled in his whole life, if only he had been permitted to reject a crown thrust upon him by the soldiery in an illegal tumult, or had been able to keep out of civil war. But the fact is a great Empire can neither be refused without danger, nor can be preserved without war.

Ithacius hastened to join the courtiers around Maximus with pleas to the conqueror to condemn the heretics by settling once and for all the affair of the Priscillianists in Spain. Maximus immediately ordered a synod to be held at Bordeaux, and gave strict instructions that all parties in the dispute should be present. It did not take the council long to condemn Instantius; but Priscillian was a different kind of person to deal with. With considerable diplomatic skill he appealed over their heads to the emperor, and they had to let him go. Bishop Priscillian with his little band of twelve male and female colleagues, arrived in Trèves to face their trial, now virtually prisoners, with the possibility of the death sentence hanging over them for a number of largely unspecified charges.

At this point, like an outraged prophet from the desert, Martin arrived in Trèves. Gregory of Tours affirms that he had been present at the Council of Bordeaux, although there is no record there of his signature; perhaps he went and refused to sign, for he had great sympathy for the so-called heretics. They seemed to him to be loyal in their devotion to the church, even if they did carry their teaching with regard to marriage too far. At any rate he had followed the prisoners to Trèves and the news of his arrival quickly spread.

He made straight for the place where Ithacius was staying, and begged him to[6]

> give up his accusations, or to implore Maximus that he should not shed the blood of the unhappy persons in question. He maintained that it was quite sufficient punishment that, having been declared heretics by a sentence of the bishops, they should have been expelled from the churches; and, that it was, besides, a foul and unheard of indignity, that a secular ruler should be judge in an ecclesiastical cause.

Ithacius, 'a bold, loquacious and extravagant man', replied sneeringly that if Martin himself was not careful, with his ridiculously ascetic ways and style of life, he might well find himself in the same case.

The new emperor and his wife, however, both devout British Christians, wished to meet the strange spiritual leader whose name was on everyone's lips both in Gaul and Britain, and invited Martin to dine with them, as no doubt all the bishops at court were wont to do in turn. Martin at first refused; he wanted to present the case for bishop Priscillian, but he certainly had no wish to join the court bishops in their ways. Eventually, however, he agreed to go.

Martin took along with him his presbyter, and in the middle of the strange banquet,[7]

> according to custom, one of the servants presented a goblet to the king. He orders it rather to be given to the very holy bishop, expecting and hoping that he should then receive the cup from his right hand. But Martin, when he had drunk, handed the goblet to his own presbyter, as thinking no one worthier to drink next to himself, and holding that it would not be right for him to prefer either the king himself, or those who were next the king, to the presbyter. And the Emperor, as well as all those who were then present, admired this conduct so much that this very thing by which they had been undervalued, gave them pleasure,

So strong was Martin's influence over the emperor that the trial was put off, and feeling that he had won the day and saved the lives of these innocent people, he set off home for Tours.

The moment he had gone the emperor acted swiftly. Priscillian's trial was arranged under Evodius, 'a man of stern and severe character', one of the emperor's close friends. Priscillian, under duress, confessed to his crimes, none of which in any case seemed to justify capital punishment, but capital punishment it was going to be. Bishop

Ithacius having hounded them down to this situation was asked to act as prosecutor in the imperial court, where the death sentence was going to be pronounced, but his stomach was turned, and he retired into the background to watch.[8]

> A certain Patricius, an advocate connected with the Treasury, was then appointed accuser by Maximus. Under him as prosecutor, Priscillian was condemned to death and along with him, Felicissimus and Armenius, who when they were clerics, had lately adopted the cause of Priscillian, and revolted from the catholics. Latronianus too, and Euchrotia were beheaded. Instantius . . . was transported to the Scilly isles which lie beyond Britain. A process was then instituted against the others in trials which followed, and Asarivus and Aurelius the deacon were condemned to be beheaded, while Tiberianus was deprived of his goods and banished. . . .

and so the sorry account goes on of the first Inquisition and its gruesome demonstration of organized catholic Christianity backed up by the imperial police in action.

The emperor was so convinced of the rightness of his actions, that with the bishops' encouragement he was preparing to send a party of tribunes to Spain, armed with absolute power to continue to search out and punish the heretics. It was even being suggested that Maximus' zeal was as a result of his casting a 'longing eye on the property of the persons in question', and that he was really after money to pay his troops.

When news was brought to Martin on the road back to Gaul of what had happened, he returned immediately to Trèves, and demanded to see the emperor. He was refused. He repeated his request the next day and it was again refused; but then help came from a quite unexpected quarter.[9]

The empress asked him to dinner, and grasping at any opportunity to prevent the tribunes from starting off he accepted the invitation. It was a strange proceeding. The empress washed the feet of the holy man with tears and wiped them with the hairs of her head. She then laid the table for him, washed his hands, and served him the food she had cooked herself, and poured his wine. Before he rose she carefully swept up the crumbs he had left. He had never dined with a woman before and the whole pantomime obviously upset him, but it achieved its purpose; he had his interview with the emperor.

The emperor finally agreed that he would stop the tribunes from leaving if Martin would join in the concelebration of the Eucharist the following day with the court bishops, who were assembled in

Trèves for the consecration of a new bishop for the city. At first Martin flatly refused. To share Eucharist with Ithacius, whose hands were stained with the blood, maliciously spilt, of fellow Christians was tantamount to being an accessory to the foul crime – the Eucharist meant people being in love and fellowship with one another – he felt no love for Ithacius or any desire whatsoever for his fellowship. But he remembered those tribunes, all packed up and ready to go, with their lists of innocent victims. In the end he gave in:[10]

> Maximus grants all his requests. On the following day the ordination of Felix as bishop was being arranged, a man undoubtedly of great sanctity, and truly worthy of being made a priest in happier times.
> Martin took part in the communion of that day, judging it better to yield for the moment, than to disregard the safety of those, over whose heads a sword was hanging. Nevertheless, although the bishops strove to the uttermost to get him to confirm the fact of his communicating by signing his name, he could not be induced to do so.

Martin left the following day in a mood of the deepest depression. He felt as if all spiritual power had left him, and that he had failed Christ. The more he thought of Ithacius and the glib sensual men of his party, whose leadership of the churches of Christ was becoming more and more the usually accepted style, the more he wondered what they had in common with Jesus. So unusually silent and sombre was his mood that his companions walked on ahead, realizing he needed to be alone with his thoughts. Soon he came to a place where the road went through a dark wood, and exhausted, he sat down to brood. All the events of the past days kept reasserting themselves, until his usual calmness was shattered. He kept wondering where he had gone wrong, and accusing himself for not taking a more active approach here and there. The darkness and the cold were signs of the enemy, who surely was behind all this confusion; when suddenly he heard someone speaking to him, and looking up he saw an angel standing there and saying 'For good cause, Martin, do you feel compunction, but you could not otherwise get out of your difficulty. Renew your virtue, resume your courage, lest you not only now expose your fame but your very salvation to danger.'[11]

When the angel had gone, Martin rose and went and rejoined the others; but he had been spiritually drained by the mental conflict, and they noticed the unusual sign of tears in his eyes. He lived sixteen years after this, but he never again attended a synod, and kept carefully aloof from all assemblies of bishops.

Martin was not the only bishop to have become sick of synods.

Their regularity and increasing frequency as the church of the fourth century had become heavily involved in synodical government for the first time, did much to destroy the pastoral role of the bishops and to turn them into official dignitaries separated from their people by the new system. The harsh experience of church politics and of the venomous and often uncharitable decisions made by synods and councils alienated some of the finest minds of the Church. One of them, Gregory, bishop of Nazianzus, could write:[12]

> my inclination is to avoid all assemblies of bishops, because I have never seen any council come to a good end, nor turn out to be a solution of evils. On the contrary it usually increases them. You always find there a love of contention and love of power . . . which beggar description.

The events leading to the execution of Priscillian bear this out, as the four councils of Rome, Saragossa, Bordeaux, and Trèves led the catholic church step by step – in spite of the lonely protest of its prophet from the caves of Marmoutier – towards the horrors of the medieval Inquisitions, and the burnings, and the pillages, and the ungodly terror, inflicted on multitudes of innocent and inoffensive people in Christ's name.

The vision of Constantine the Great was taking firm shape in those councils, for even whilst they were conducting their business a new emperor, Theodosius I was making his way to the imperial throne. He eventually conquered Magnus Maximus in the year AD 388 and assumed the title of Augustus of both East and West; he was the last effective emperor to do so.

Falling sick shortly after his coronation as Emperor of the East in AD 380, he had been baptized. When he recovered, he issued an edict which was to form the basis of his future rule both of East and West;[13]

> It is our pleasure that all the nations, which are governed by our Clemency and Moderation, should steadfastly adhere to the religion which was taught by St Peter to the Romans. . . . We authorize the followers of this doctrine to assume the title of Catholic Christians; and as we judge that all others are extravagant madmen, we brand them with the infamous name of heretics; and declare that their conventicles shall no longer usurp the respectable appellation of churches . . . besides the condemnation of divine justice, they must expect to suffer the severe penalties which our Authority, guided by heavenly wisdom, shall think proper to inflict upon them.

Though Theodosius' rule would not last long, and the hordes of the barbarians would come soon, pouring over the borders of the empire, it was a dream the catholic church never forgot.

Sitting there in the dark wood Martin did well to weep.

14

With the thought still rankling in his mind of bishop Priscillian and his pathetic companions, Martin, at the age of sixty-five, made his way back to Tours, deeply distressed in spite of the comfort of his angelic visitation.

The only way he knew how to work the horror of it out of his system was to return with renewed vigour to his prayer in his cell and to his pastoral ministry. For those last sixteen years he was engaged in the most fruitful of all the periods of his ministry; for during that time he was laying down in a very tentative and speculative way the foundations of the parochial system, one of the most enduring and creative social institutions the world has known. Before Martin's ministry, no parochial system had existed in the church or the state, certainly not in the countryside, and the system in Europe and Britain can clearly be traced back to him.

The picture that has emerged in this study of the church of the first four centuries, is that the day to day pastoral work devolved upon the bishop and his presbyters and deacons who worked with him as a group or team, often living with him in the bishop's house.

Whenever a congregation started to form, usually in a town or city, but sometimes in a large village, a bishop was chosen as its pastor, assisted by a deacon; as soon as the congregation grew to any size, the bishop would ordain presbyters elected from the congregation, who might well be engaged in work or business in the community. They would as a group assist him at the Eucharist, provide a consultative council, help him in the pastorate and deputize for him when he was ill or away. There was no suggestion that the presbyter might work on his own in forming or serving a congregation, for this seemed contradictory not only to scripture but also to good order and unity.

Cyprian of Carthage, writing somewhere around AD 250, had

summed up the conception in one short phrase – '*Unus in Ecclesia ad tempus sacerdos*' – one bishop for one diocese or parish; and even as he wrote he was conscious that behind him in the north African hinterland there were some 300 bishops, each in charge of his own small parish or diocese, for these words were used interchangeably for the undefined sphere of influence of a local bishop.

So deeply rooted was this conception of the ministry of the church as a team or group that at Rome, for instance, where the central congregation had become so large that twenty-five churches had had to be built each with a staff of five or six presbyters, the work of these men was confined at first to preparing people living in the nearby streets for baptism. The pope himself not only conducted all baptisms but also every Eucharist, presiding over it in each church in turn. At the end of the service at the church where he was, the bread and wine that he had consecrated in the presence of the people was carried by acolytes to all the other churches for distribution by the presbyters there to the congregations.[1]

By the same token, when congregations started to form in the surrounding small townships of Ostia, Tusculum, Albano and the like, all about twenty-five kilometres away from the city, then it was natural to provide each one with a bishop, and these bishops formed a kind of local synod with the bishop of Rome as Metropolitan.

As it was at Rome so it was almost everywhere, the same principles were involved, and when the Council of Sardica in AD 343 stated that 'permission is not to be given to ordain a bishop either in any village, or in an unimportant city, for which one presbyter suffices,'[2] whilst they were trying to upgrade the status of the bishop, they were not envisaging the presbyter acting unilaterally or celebrating the liturgy apart from the bishop.

So it was at Tours. The large influx of candidates for baptism under the influence of the various benevolent imperial decrees and the strange and dynamic leadership of Martin, would not lead to the breaking down of the eucharistic congregation gathered round the bishop, presbyters and deacons, even if it meant enlarging the cathedral or building other churches in the town.

In a town such as Amboise, eighteen or so kilometres upstream from Tours, as already mentioned Martin had established the presbyter Marcellus and a group of monks from Marmoutier, whose task was to demolish through prayer or any other means that came to hand, the large idol-temple 'constructed of the most polished stones and furnished with turrets'.[3] Their task was to continue the round of prayer and study as at Marmoutier, and Martin himself from time to time would do the day's march out there to visit them, spend some time with them, celebrate Eucharist, and confer with them about the work.

There were five other chosen centres probably all founded by Martin and visited by him in much the same way, Sonnay, Langeais, Chisseaux, St Pierre de Tournon and Candes, some of them much more than a day's march from Tours.[4]

These centres were monasteries founded in all probability on or near the sites of desecrated pagan shrines, and in founding his centres in this way Martin displayed considerable pastoral insight.[5] The population of the Gallic countryside was widely scattered in small farms, hamlets and villages, whose inhabitants would come together to the well-known shrines for festivals; there they would now meet, even before their shrine was desecrated as at Amboise, a group of dedicated Christian men or even women, living the Christian life with all the intensity of their ascetic training. After the destruction of the shrine and the building of a church for worship, which the people themselves would sometimes help to build, they would come to it for worship, and those who wished for instruction for baptism. The service would probably have been something similar to the service for the catechumens and not proceed to the Eucharist unless the bishop were present.

When Martin founded churches further away from Tours than he was likely to be able to visit fairly frequently, other provision had to be made. In the struggles of the primitive church to deal with this problem of inevitable expansion, laterally as it were, as has been seen at Rome, the bishop in the central town would consecrate a leading member of the congregation presented to him by the congregation in the large village or town to be its local bishop. These local bishops in the countryside were often called in the ancient church, *chorepiscopoi*, or country-bishops. Discussion will always continue about the precise function of these men, but there seems little doubt but that they were properly consecrated bishops, who were charged with setting up a small team around them of presbyters and deacon, on the model of the large town, to serve their district. They were to maintain a close working relationship with the bishop of the town or city that founded them, and were free to exercise every episcopal function, except that of ordination to any office above that of reader.[6]

Nowhere does Sulpitius state that Martin was consecrating such country-bishops in the parish centres he was creating at some distance from Tours, but bearing in mind the general practice of the contemporary Church and the fact that there were many country bishops still working in Gaul as late as the ninth century, it seems more than likely that he was. Late in his life people had come to look on Marmoutier as a school for bishops, and his visit to Candes some fifty kilometres away, where he eventually died, seemed to imply the presence of quite a considerable group of presbyters and deacons, and such a presbyterium that far away from Tours without a bishop would have appeared at that time quite irregular.

Martin returned from the miserable visit to Trèves to this kind of work of establishing and maintaining the church life at Tours and in the countryside around, working from the base of his wooden hut under the cliffs at Marmoutier. It is difficult to see how he managed to marry his busy pastoral and apostolic life with his chosen vocation of solitary prayer and fasting, but it seems he managed the rhythm of anvil-ding and well directed blow with stern success. It is even possible to piece together roughly how the routine worked, in spite of its somewhat spontaneous nature.

From mid-November until the end of December he would visit, like many bishops apparently did, around his diocese, travelling sometimes by boat up and down the river, but more often on foot or riding on a mule or donkey; Sulpitius describes it: 'about the middle of the winter he came to a certain parish, according to the usual custom for the bishops to visit the churches in the diocese';[7] and again, it was on 11 November that he died at the beginning of one of these circular tours.

Always he travelled with companions, members of his presbyterium or fellow hermits from Marmoutier, though it seems he often walked alone and away from them, deep in prayer. When he walked with them they learnt a lot from his observations on country scenes, and of the genuine sympathy of his character, as when they came across the hunt, with the dogs coursing, or chasing, the hare. As he watched the poor creature doubling to and fro, exhausted, he called the dogs off in an authoritative voice and the hare seeing its chance at the momentary check, made its escape.[8] The weather up to Epiphany time (6 January) is not unusually cold in this region, and work on the farms was slack so that the people were free to talk with him if they desired it; and at night the *secretaria* of the churches or monasteries had fires lit, and some even a hypocaust.[9]

From January, when the roads became impassable and the river was in spate, he would surely retire to Tours, there to winter and keep the fast of Lent, to help in the preparation of baptism candidates and to celebrate the Paschal feast.

The summer would be spent on the long journeys to the court at Trèves, with their accompanying missionary labours, or attending to the affairs of the church as they affected him outside Tours for there seems some indication that through the reorganization of the provinces undertaken by the emperor Gratian, Tours had become the capital city of a wide district, and this could well have resulted in his fellow bishops seeking his counsel on their problems, as their metropolitan. By September he was back again at Tours for another period of complete seclusion in his cell before the winter's rounds began again.

Of Martin as preacher, Sulpitius keeps a low profile which was unusual for him, and his silence is eloquent. Martin was not a great preacher like Ambrose or Augustine, on whose words everyone hung. As befitted a soldier his sermons were direct, enthusiastic and didactic, the sermons of the humble parish priest who was quite prepared to leave knotty theological problems to people like his master Hilary. His heart ruled his speech rather than his head; and on one occasion he found himself in dialogue with brother hermits, saying that he was sure that if the Devil repented of all the evil he had done God would forgive him, a statement which would have raised a few eyebrows among the theologians of the East.

Sulpitius as if to draw a gentle veil over this important part of Martin's ministry describes a day when they persuaded him to talk about the second coming of Christ. The old man gave an interesting enough talk, but with no rhetorical embellishments; Sulpitius carefully recorded it as remembered and retold by the Gaul, but then in his dialogue he caused the boy to enter with the news that the local presbyter Refrigius had called to pay his respects, and they never did get back to talking about Martin's sermon.[10]

As they grow old, men often begin to worry about their declining powers and their waning virility; the death of friends reminds them that they themselves must leave soon; and the readjustment to a quiet life of retirement and seclusion often within an ever-narrowing prison, of power to enjoy the senses, fills them with a horror of boredom and frustration.

Perhaps the reason why so many of the hermits lived to such a great age on their one dish of herbs a day, interspersed with days of fasting, no toilet facilities or medical help, and clothes that were rarely repaired or washed, was because they had faced the situation of growing old and diminishment for a very long time and embraced it with pleasure when it came.

It is noticeable, for instance, in the case of Antony, who lived to the age of 105, that the total repression of his sexual drive, as in the case of many recluses, led to violent sexual imaginations and a marked tetchiness in middle age; but old age brought relief and that particular kind of blandness that is the mark of holiness.

So with Martin, when Sulpitius found him sitting outside his hut in the last years of his life; 'no one ever saw him enraged or excited, or lamenting or laughing; he was always the same, displaying a kind of heavenly happiness.'[11]

Partly, too, this serenity was due to the knowledge that old age was a kind of gentle passion, or suffering; a white martyrdom to be welcomed as warmly as the martyr's delirious embracing of sudden death in the arena.[12]

> Wholly given to thee I will fulfil whatever duties thou dost assign me, and I will serve under thy standard as long as thou shalt prescribe. Yes, although release is sweet to an old man after lengthened toil, yet my mind is a conqueror over my years, and I am not one to yield to old age.

Now in his eighties, Martin was consciously drawing towards the end of his life and he had chosen a successor to put before the people for election, after he had gone. His name was Bricius or Brice, a young man who had become very close to Martin, and who had more or less grown up from his youth in the monastery.

Brice had, it seems, been around on his travels with Martin and had come to value the high style in which many of the bishops were then living. To Brice, Martin's style of living was plainly ridiculous and only brought scorn on him and the church, when compared with the style of bishop Ambrose of Milan for instance, or bishop Ithacius and his colleagues at the court. Every man had the right to enjoy himself, if only a little, even a bishop, and this ludicrous idea of a bishop living in a wooden hut, in the midst of a shanty town, with no servants, dreadfully untidy, and spending all his day with the Bible was despicable.

Brice had other ideas. When the old man died he was going to organize things on a different basis. He would sort out the crowds of gaping pilgrims, make them pay in various ways for seeing the old man's three-legged stool or touching his tomb, and generally get the sort of cash flow going that ought to have been achieved years before. Then he could live in style as a prince of the church like the others, consort with kings and emperors and their wives, attend great gatherings of well-dressed bishops, and leave his mark on the world. Of course, like the holy man Ambrose, he did not intend to let his inner and spiritual life diminish in any way; at least he had learnt the importance of that from Martin. He intended to have the best of both worlds.

From time to time as Brice watched Martin sitting on his three-legged stool in the sun on summer days outside his hut, he would think to himself that the crazy old man might just as well hand over the reins to him now, and appoint him as his coadjutor to run things for him as some bishops were doing in spite of the regulations.

When such a mood came over him, he would storm up to the hut and egged on by boys climbing on the cliffs above, who loved this scene whenever it happened, he would explode;[13]

with trembling lips and a changing countenance, pale with rage, he rolled forth the words of sin, asserting that he was a holier man than Martin, who had brought him up, inasmuch as from his earliest years he had grown up in a monastery, amid the sacred institutions of the Church, while Martin had at first, as he could not deny, been tarnished with the life of a soldier, and had now entirely sunk into dotage by means of his baseless superstitions and ridiculous fancies about visions.

That was exceedingly hurtful talk, for outside Marmoutier there were many responsible and godly church leaders who felt the same; and even the pope of Rome, Siricius had issued statements to the effect that old soldiers who had continued to serve in the army after their baptism should not be made bishops, especially those who pretended to extremes of holiness.[14]

Martin listened to all this outwardly unperturbed, and when later Brice crept back to apologize and others came to enquire how long he was going to put up with such contemptuous barracking, he would say: 'If Christ bore with Judas, why should I not bear with Brice?'

Death when it came, came swiftly. He died in harness at the beginning of one of his winter rounds of parish visitations, on the eleventh day of the eleventh month in the year AD 397 in the eighty-first year of his age.

News had reached him of a quarrel that had broken out in the presbyterium at Candes, and he was determined to go there to settle it if he could. The shortest way to Candes is by water, downstream from Tours and it is pleasing to reflect on him drifting downstream on a barge with his companions towards the confluence of the two rivers, the Vienne and the Loire, at Candes, where they meet to form a large placid stretch of water beloved of holidaymakers.

His mind full of the mystery of evil that makes men quarrel rather than live at peace, he watched the waterfowl fishing and noted their repeated dives under the surface for their prey: 'the demons are like that,' he said, 'voracious, they will never be satisfied', and he shouted across to them. To everyone's surprise the birds took flight at the word of command like soldiers and moved off in formation. It seemed a good omen; but the old man was exhausted, and over the whole journey there was an air of finality.[15]

They arrived at Candes, went up to the church and installed Martin in the *secretarium*. Overawed by his condition the brothers patched up their quarrel; but when it was time to go home, he could not move. He had a high fever and lay on the floor on his back and would not be touched. He would accept no straw to lie on, but only his familiar sackcloth and ashes.

Looking at his weeping companions, he suddenly longed to go on living, there was so much still to do in the battle against Satan, and they heard him say: 'O Lord if I am still necessary to thy people, I do not shrink from toil;[16] thy will be done.'

He lingered on for a few days, and when his presbyters around him suggested that they might lift him and change his position, he refused; he wanted, he said, his eyes to be fixed towards heaven as he knew he had not long to live. Then suddenly he swore furiously: 'Why do you stand there you bloody monster? You shall find nothing in me, you deadly one: Abraham's bosom is about to receive me. . . .' and he was gone.

It is difficult these days to find Candes, especially if you are on foot, but the effort is worth making. The long walk from Chinon, where the woods stretch far and wide, gives you ample time for reflection. When eventually you arrive, turn down to the right and follow the lane to the water's edge, and, looking over the broad expanse of calm water, think of that barge that pulled in here 1,600 years ago. Then make your way past the presbytery up to the graceful medieval church on the hillside and find the side chapel on the north.

There on the floor you will see a large black stone slab, with this simple legend:

ICI MARTIN EST MORT

Along with Pope John XXIII, who struggled out here to pray because of his lifetime devotion and interest in Martin, it is difficult in the quiet stillness to remain unmoved.[17]

> *You are not here to verify*
> *Instruct yourself, or inform curiosity*
> *Or carry report. You are here to kneel*
> *Where prayer has been valid. And prayer is more*
> *Than an order of words, the conscious occupation*
> *Of the praying mind, or the sound of the voice praying.*
> *And what the dead had no speech for, when living,*
> *They can tell you, being dead: the communication*
> *Of the dead is tongued with fire beyond the language of the living.*

Part Four

The cult

15

The men of Tours, probably well-led by Brice, snatched the body of Martin from under the noses of their rivals, the men of Poitiers, while they were sleeping. They passed it out of the window to colleagues waiting below. It was placed in a barge which was hastily pushed off and started the long struggle up against the stream to Tours, in the middle of the night.[1]

No sooner had Martin died than the men of Poitiers who had come to his deathbed to take the body back to their town, because of his ten happy years at Ligugé, started a violent argument with the men of Tours, until at last they had all fallen asleep, giving the vigilant men of Tours their chance.

As they struggled upstream with their precious burden, the men of Tours had cause to be proud of their opportunism for they had on board with them something that would bring them fame, glory and thousands of pilgrims from all over the world, to say nothing of a consequent boom in their trade. And, of course, they were right, for one of the most successful and persistent cults in Christendom was to grow up around Martin's body, and to continue down to this very day.

The people of Tours gave Martin's body a glorious funeral when it arrived, over which, as was fitting, Sulpitius let all his powers of rhetoric, trained for just such an occasion as this, have full play:[2]

> Let there be compared with this spectacle, I will not say the worldly pomp of a funeral, but even of a triumph. . . .
> Let your worldly great men lead before their chariots captives with their hands bound behind their backs. Those accompanied the body of Martin, who, under his guidance had overcome the world, etc.

It was fine stuff, sonorous and elegant, as befitted the placing of a hero's body in its catafalque, where thousands would press forward to touch it. But it was no good, the stern and uncompromising spirituality of Martin was not fitted to these extravagances and all that followed from them in Tours.

Martin's unique style of Christian life was to blossom elsewhere, in the severe lives of the young noblemen and army officers whom he had trained at Marmoutier and who were becoming bishops of many dioceses of Gaul; but especially in the foundation of the monastery in the island of Lérins in the Mediterranean and in the mission to the peoples of the islands of Britain, 400 kilometres away.

Honoratus, the founder of the great monastery at Lérins was born in the decade after the consecration of Martin as bishop of Tours in AD 370. Even as a child he had withdrawn from the games of his fellows, and having cut his hair like Martin's monks, would go off to be by himself. In AD 390 he and his brother set off on a pilgrimage round southern Gaul, Italy and Greece, in the company of an aged Christian, Caprais, in order to seek for guidance about the ascetic life. They eventually passed through Nola, where they visited Paulinus, and it is scarcely credible that they did not have a chance of reading there the recently published *Life of St Martin* by Sulpitius, of which Paulinus was so full; besides which they would have many chances of finding out what the saint and his community were like at Marmoutier from descriptions by Paulinus of his visit there.[3]

After leaving Paulinus, Honoratus, accompanied by his aged companion Caprais, found the deserted island of Lérins, off the bay of Cannes, at one time dedicated as a place of heathen rites, and as Martin had done at Gallinaria, they set up a hermitage there, with the encouragement of Leontius, the bishop at Fréjus on the mainland. Honoratus was soon surrounded by fellow hermits for whom he built huts, and he tried to train them on the same lines as he had heard Martin had done. The monastery came to have a fame as wide as Marmoutier, and indeed, when Martin died seems to have taken over its work of training young men of noble rank for posts of spiritual leadership in Gaul in the dark days of the invasions; for bishop Brice was hardly the type of man to attract young ascetics, seeking evangelical perfection, to Tours.

There was, however, another powerful and direct line of spiritual succession from Martin, which was developing in the British Isles, always known as the religious retreat and training ground of the religious leaders of the Celtic peoples.[4] The story of its development is one that can only be told haltingly, and be pieced together from many different sources, demanding that most difficult of all research, where disciplines so near and yet so far apart as that of the archaeologist, the historian and the enthusiastic amateur with his hunches are concerned; but it has about it all the excitement of a search barely begun.

Starting from Marmoutier the line of succession of Martinian spirituality leads to Tara, to Iona, to the Whithorn in Galloway, to the Farne islands and to many an English and Welsh parish church, under which lies hidden all unsuspected, a desecrated Romano-Celtic shrine, or the floor of the *triclinium* or dining room of a Roman villa, that had been used for Christian house worship.[5]

The history of the coming of Christianity to Britain in the first three centuries is very obscure. Understandably there are few archaeo-logical remains, as Christian worship all through this period would have been conducted in houses and not normally have been open to the public. Apart from the isolated case of Alban's death at Verulamium around AD 208-9, it seems that Britain had been more or less free from the full blast of the great persecutions, and this would imply that the Christian people there were a small and easily contained group. It would also seem to imply that they were drawn largely from the aristocratic and officer classes, for they would know how to protect themselves through influence at court, a not altogether difficult task at this time as the emperor Constantius I, who was staying then in Britain, was known to have a secret sympathy with the Christian sufferers.

The frequent references to the presence of a number of Christian bishops from Britain at various councils of the church in Gaul gives a somewhat misleading impression of size at first sight as the tendency is immediately to assume that each bishop ruled over a large and well-developed diocese, whereas, as has been already pointed out, it could rather mean that there were about half a dozen congregations, not all of them large, in the main towns and cities, with a few villa churches dependent upon them, where wealthy Christian people lived in the countryside.

In the account of Martin's life, two British Christians have already made their appearance – Magnus Maximus and his wife. Maximus had already served for two years as a general in Britain, when Martin was consecrated bishop of Tours in AD 370. He was a Spaniard and a protégé of the emperor Theodosius, who was well known for his championship of the catholic Christian faith. The whole attitude of Maximus throughout the story is typical of the aristocratic Christians of Britain, strongly catholic in their beliefs, who, now that Christianity, the Emperor's religion, was become respectable, were decorating the floors of the dining rooms of their villas, where Christian worship took place, with Christian motifs. Beautifully wrought in mosaic, such as that at Hinton St Mary in Dorset, the work carried out by the local firm at Dorchester, it might have the head of Christ in the centre, with the chi-rho monogram as background, with all around the figures of the animals of the chase.

Theirs was a domestic form of Christianity, thoroughly suited to the weekly round of an important Roman household, where it would not be considered improper to gaze down on the floor during service time on sunny autumn days, whilst the presbyter said the prayers and lessons, or the bishop celebrated Eucharist, with the thought of the afternoon's hunting strongly in mind.

Although perhaps a few of the slaves and freemen from the farm with their wives and children might be present at the service, the majority would be involved in the worship of the local Celtic deity at the square stone temple on the hill. Provided by the Romans, and including their own gods, it is not easy to understand who conducted the worship there, perhaps the people themselves, but the shrines were much used and cared for until late in the fourth century, and the Christians in the villa would not have dreamt of trying to disturb them or convert the worshippers to Christianity.

But then from AD 370 onwards, as there are so many small indications to show, something happened to the Christians in Britain, and even if Magnus Maximus for instance, when he became emperor, retained his old aristocratic Christianity, his wife had completely changed. Her reaction to meeting Martin was so markedly different to that of[6] her husband that it needs an explanation beyond that of mere spontaneous feminine admiration. Her whole conduct, extravagantly washing his feet, lying on the floor and listening to every word he said, cooking and clearing away the meal for him, all indicate that she was not meeting Martin for this first time as a stranger, but as the hero and father figure of a religious movement long known to her, and whose principles she wholeheartedly accepted.

Her conduct implies that someone had come to her in Britain from Marmoutier and completely changed her Christian outlook; she was no longer the staid aristocratic Roman matron, but a devout follower of the ascetics, burning with Christian ardour in the pursuit of perfection. She was not the only one to experience this kind of conversion in Britain at this time, and the inescapable impression is left that there was, in the last years of the fourth century in Britain, no less than some sort of mission inspired from Marmoutier to Britain, which changed the old aristocratic family Christianity of the villa into a thoroughgoing monastic church with a large following in the space of forty or fifty years.

One of the first to be completely captivated by these anonymous missionaries was a brilliant young Briton, Pelagius. Somewhere between AD 370 and 380 he was converted to the ascetic way of life, for by the year AD 380 he was teaching in Rome. His teaching had the simplicity and forthrightness of the kind of demands Martin made on his followers; and of his indebtedness to Martin's teaching there can be no doubt. 'Membership of the Church', he taught, 'did not involve half measures'; and 'since perfection is possible for man, it is obligatory.'

As a dedicated 'servant of God', though never a hermit, he visited Paulinus of Nola, even travelling to Bethlehem to meet Jerome, and seemed to set himself in true Celtic style to reform the church single-handed on Martinian lines, a task that made him thoroughly unpopular.

Whoever those anonymous missionaries were, they certainly wielded a wide influence, and caused a considerable disturbance in Britain, and by the year AD 396, a year before Martin's death, the situation had become so difficult that the Christian community in Britain invited one of Martin's friends, Victricius, the missionary bishop of Rouen, to come over to Britain to help sort them out.[7]

In view of what has been written here of Martin's lifestyle it is possible to make a guess as to what the disturbance that had got so far out of hand was, especially as everyone felt they should get one of Martin's friends to sort it out. The indigenous church in Britain, aristocratic and without drive to seek conversions from the native population had become content with the pleasant intimacy of their house worship; it was the kind of Christianity being taught by Ausonius, gentle, well-integrated into the formalities of Roman home life, and making no great devotional demands.

The sudden arrival into such a worshipping group one Sunday of two wild-looking men, dirty and dishevelled, their hair matted and cut in such a way as to make them frighten the children, looking pale and exhausted and yet with eyes ablaze with some crazy zeal for Christ, and bearing in their hands their 'letters pacifical' from the famous bishop of Tours demanding that they be offered hospitality, would certainly of itself cause some disturbance.

When the truth dawned that they had come to demand of all the hunting and fishing Christians that they should forsake their worldly ways and follow their own extraordinary way of life, giving their wealth away and their fine food, and living on one handful of herbs a day, the local Christians would feel that it was time the bishop or someone took control and ordered them out; except that here and there someone like Maximus' wife, would see the point and want to know more.

When the two started arguing with the local slaves and peasants at the shrine on the hill, and actually began to pull the tiles off the roof, so that all the farm workers were up in arms, it was time to use physical restraint. And then to be told, as Christian people too, that far from stopping them it was their duty to help, for did they not know of the emperor's laws ordering all shrines to be deserted and thrown down? A difficult situation had indeed arisen, and when Victricius came and eventually sorted things out as best he could, he left the British people in no doubt, judging by his exuberance on his return to Rouen, that the monks were right and should be followed.

From then on (AD 396) the campaign would really have got under way, and there are a number of pointers both archaeological and historic that suggest how it happened.

Both the churches mentioned by the Venerable Bede as having been standing in Britain since the time of the Roman occupation are dedicated to St Martin. Could one of them provide the name of one of those anonymous missionaries of the last decades of the fourth century?

Bede, writing in AD 730, mentions that a Briton called Nynian,[8] had, long before the middle of the sixth century, gone to Rome where he had been taught the faith and then returned as bishop to Galloway where he built a conspicuous stone church, an unusual thing in Britain at that time, and named it after St Martin of Tours. A much later biographer, Aelred of Rievaulx, writing in the twelfth century, yet confident that he had made the most careful research tells the story of how, as Nynian returned from Rome, he visited Martin at Marmoutier and was provided with masons to help him build his church, which he ultimately named the Candida Casa, the White Castle, or Whithorn.

The relation between the site and St Martin of Tours has had a long and disputed history, but both the site of the church and its cave associated with Nynian some five kilometres away in a small bay, near a clear, rushing stream, have a strong feel of an attempt to recreate Marmoutier in this desolate spot.

Bede also records how there was on the east side of the city of Canterbury a 'church built in honour of St Martin a great while ago, whilst the Romans still dwelt in Britain'[9] and that King Ethelbert the Saxon restored it, along with a number of similar churches, after his marriage to the Frankish princess Bertha. In a well-argued case which largely remains unchallenged the Victorian archaeologist, Charles F. Routledge claims that the nave of the church as it stands is mainly of late Roman date, that it was originally part of a villa, and had association with a pagan shrine.[10] Corroborative evidence of a vigorous Christian community in Canterbury has recently come to light, which includes a number of late fourth-century silver spoons marked with the chi-rho monogram, a strange implement also marked with the chi-rho, and two silver donatives, which suggest the presence in the group, of soldiers or officials.[11]

Whilst the custom of the naming of churches after saints has changed considerably over the years, it seems that the earlier the date of the dedication of the church the more likely is it to have been named after a person still then living, for any idea of formal canonization procedures or dedication ceremonies in this period must be discounted, and the title Saint was one often bandied about in letters to bishops by the imperial authorities, even when their recipients were clearly unworthy of mention in such a context. The idea that any Christian group at work in Britain at this time, inspired by the example of Marmoutier, would be inclined to name some of the churches they built after St Martin is certainly one that needs to be reckoned with.

The Roman Christian villa at Lullingstone provides another most interesting example of what was happening in Britain around AD 370. This large villa was laid out on the banks of the little river Darent, near Sevenoaks in Kent, somewhere in the first century AD, and over the years was added to and enlarged. In the fourth century, around AD 300, a Romano-Celtic burial shrine was built on a terrace behind the villa. Somewhere around AD 330 superb mosaic floors were laid, and the villa was enlarged. Then, suddenly, between AD 364 and 378,[12] the owner and his family embraced Christianity, and the whole character of the villa began to change, ceasing to be a farm and becoming more of a Christian meeting place. The temple mausoleum was destroyed completely, even with digging under the foundations, and a three-roomed house-church was built on the first floor, with a door that opened towards the outside on the north allowing people to enter, without disturbing those who lived in the villa.

The wall paintings of the *orantes* which showed six human figures with their hands outstretched in prayer have a close affinity with the style of painting used by Sulpitius and Paulinus in adorning their villas which they were transforming into basilicas for public worship in France and Italy; and further interest is added by the fact that churches, now of medieval construction, at the entrances to the estate, at Eynsford and Chelsfield are named after St Martin.

At Maiden castle in Dorset one of the largest Celtic hill-forts in Britain, there was a 'great idol temple, built up with labour',[13] which for the Christians of Britain clearly proved, like the shrine at Amboise, very difficult to destroy. There was an active group of Christians at Dorchester, five kilometres away, where silver spoons similar to those at Canterbury, only marked with the fish symbol, have been found. The shrine was a Celtic stronghold and was repaired as late as between AD 380 and 400. Over against the temple, Sir Mortimer Wheeler identified a small rough-hewn building of almost 'ostentatious barbarism',[14] and its purpose seemed to him impossibly obscure. To readers of Sulpitius, however, its strong similarity to the situation at Amboise is evident, where the presbyter Marcellus and a few fellow hermits were lodged near the shrine to destroy it. At all events, when the crisis was over, and the shrine demolished, everyone left the windy height and moved down into the valley below, where they founded a village which to this day is named Martinstown.

There is an extraordinarily strong connection between St Martin's name and Roman sites throughout Britain, as for instance at Dover, a whole town dedicated to St Martin; at Herne near Reculver in Kent; at Chichester, Colchester, Chester to name only a few where there are, or were, prominent sites connected with him; and the whole connection opens up possibilities for a fruitful exploration, which could shed fresh light on this age of British history where every scrap of information is valuable.

When it is asked why there is not more archaeological evidence of destroyed Romano-Celtic shrines in Britain, the answer again is to be found by reference to the practice started by Martin, for 'wherever he destroyed heathen temples, there he used immediately to build either churches or monasteries'.[15] Many of those desecrated shrines are nestling snugly under the chancels of England's ancient medieval parish churches, with very few clues that they are there apart from their ancient dedication name. One has recently been uncovered at Stone near Faversham, beside Watling Street, where the temple formed the chancel of a medieval church, now in ruins; and an interesting example of a villa church changing into a parish church is to be found at the little church of St Oswald at Widford near Burford in Oxfordshire. During renovations in 1904 the tesselated pavement of a Roman villa was found underneath the chancel, showing from how early a date so many of the sites of England's parish churches were occupied for religious purposes.

On that famous occasion when Victricius returned in such high spirits to Rouen from his visit to Britain in AD 396, he was quite carried away in his oration and described his typical congregation as he had formed it at Rouen. It is a description that would fit any congregation living in the mainstream of Martinian spirituality. By the time the legions were departing from Britain in AD 420, it would have fitted any British congregation in contrast to the more domestic style of its aristocratic predecessor. As they walked into church, the congregation was led in by monks in their black robes, followed by the children, the virgins, the widows, the continents (the servants of God vowed to sexual continence), and finally the rump of the ordinary worshippers mixed in with the catechumens, and presumably the pathetic group of the *energoumenoi*. The British church was a large and vigorous church, but it was based on the devotion of monks and hermits, and the members of the congregations would have had, as they did at Marmoutier, to fend for themselves pastorally, except in cases of emergency.

Within this type of congregation there grew up in the first years of the fifth century, on the West coast of Britain a young boy named Patrick, the son of a deacon of the church, who, after many adventures, was to take the Martinian style of spirituality to the very last stronghold of the pagan Celts in Ireland. He was captured and taken there by pirates as a child, and growing up, escaped and journeyed across Gaul – now devastated – to Lérins. There he trained himself as a monk and planned to return to take the Christian religion to Ireland. He did not begin his mission to Ireland until he was sixty years of age, and in an incredibly short period of time won the hearts of the Irish people for Christ. His writings have a rough simplicity that explain why the tradition has been so strong that in some way he was physically related to Martin and his fight with the Druids of Tara is in the main-stream of the unarmed single combat so familiar in Martin's life.

The ancient religion of the Druids was now finally replaced with the way of primitive Christianity as Martin had set it out. Not only in Ireland, but in Wales and Scotland, great monasteries sprang up, modelled on Marmoutier, and there is evidence that Sulpitius' *Life of St Martin* was widely read and followed.[16] The monasteries may have been rough and ready and very crudely built, often composed of a circle of beehive wattle huts round a central stone building, but, whilst a dark desert of confusion reigned in Gaul, it was they, with the fierceness of their uncompromising devotion, who kept alive not only the spirit but the practice of civilization almost as a by-product of their spiritual industry.

Perhaps the last word from them must come from him who was the very epitome of Martinian devotion – Columba of Iona. The ancient tradition tells how in his youth he went to Tours and brought away the gospel book that lay on Martin's breast and left it in Derry.[17] A passionate Christian and a monk, in his enthusiasm for the scriptures he unintentionally started a fierce tribal battle in which many were killed, and as a result exiled himself for ever from the Ireland he loved. Setting sail with twelve companions in May AD 563, he sailed until he could see the coast of his beloved Ireland no more, and there on an island off the coast of Scotland, where the Druids had reigned for years, the island of Iona, they settled. They drove the Druids out, and making for themselves a circle of beehive huts around a wooden church and refectory, the whole enclosed as befitted an encampment of Christ's soldiers with a vallum or rampart of earth and stones, they set out to recapitulate the experience of Marmoutier in this desolate spot. This little enclosure, where a fine Celtic cross to St Martin stands today, became a vital centre from which not only Columba but later many of his followers, set out on Martin-style missionary campaigns to Britain, Gaul and some even say America, in their boats made of skins; always full of Celtic dash and imagination, and ready to engage with Satan and his devils in personal unarmed combat.

Columba had the special gift of poesy, in which surely he distilled the gospel according to St Martin.

That I might bless the Lord
Who conserves all;
Heaven with its countless bright orders,
Land, strand and flood;
That I might search the books all
That would be good for my soul;
At times kneeling to beloved heaven;
At times at psalm singing;
At times contemplating the king of heaven,
Holy the chief;
At times at work without compulsion;
This would be delightful.
At times picking kelp from the rocks;
At times at fishing;
At times giving food to the poor;
At times in a solitary cell,
The best advice to me has been granted.[18]

I adore not the voice of birds
Nor chance, nor the love of a son or a wife,
My DRUID IS CHRIST, *the Son of God,*
The Son of Mary, the Great Abbot,
The Father, the Son and the Holy Spirit.[19]

16

If Martin's spirituality, based on the stern and uncompromising life of the Christians of the early centuries AD had found a temporary home in Ireland, Wales and the islands of Iona and Lérins, the Christian church in Gaul after Martin's death had but a short breathing space before the barbarian hordes came pouring across Europe in the winter of 406, leaving behind them a trail of misery and destruction. 'In a miraculously short time – about fifty years – the classical world was overrun. Only its bleached bones stood out against the Mediterranean sky.'[1]

The people of the church of Tours felt, however, comparatively safe, for not only had they a well-fortified city, but, far more importantly, through the dexterity of their team at the funeral, they had possession of the priceless treasure of the body of Martin. It is difficult for us now to understand their feeling of assurance, which certainly had, as subsequent events showed, ample justification; and some explanation of the reason for it must be attempted, for it explains much that was taking place in the church at the time.

In the first three centuries of the church's life, the bodies of the saints, especially of those who had been martyred had always been venerated. At the place of their burial, on the anniversary of their death, the local Christian group kept their memory alive by celebrating Eucharist, followed by an *Agape* or love feast. It was a memorial act of veneration for the dead saint's acts of heroic sacrifice, made all the more vivid by the thought that the remains of their actual physical bodies, that had borne the brunt of the enemy's attack, were but a few feet away; it helped to make the sense of spiritual fellowship almost palpable, and added force to the joyful acknowledgment in the liturgy, of the living presence of the saints. This kind of veneration Martin was the first to acknowledge, especially for the sense of continuity it provided with the primitive Church and its ways; and

Gregory of Tours, his successor and admirer recalls how he caused the body of the first bishop of Tours, Gatien, who had survived the rigours of the persecutions, to be buried in a tomb in the church in Tours.[2]

In the fourth century, however, this pious custom of veneration began to take on, all of a sudden, a quite new aspect, which seemed, as in so many other changes of emphasis in the church at this period, to be due primarily to the activity of the emperor Constantine the Great and other members of his family.

The story went that the emperor Constantine, after the triumph of the Council of Nicaea had sent his mother, the empress Helena, to superintend the cleansing of the sites of the Lord's crucifixion and resurrection, which had been defiled with pagan monuments. With the assistance of a local Jew, she had been led to a spot where the crosses were supposed to be buried. Digging revealed the three crosses, complete with Pilate's placard that had fallen off, lying beside them on the ground. Uncertain as to which of the three was the cross on which Jesus had suffered, the empress caused a noble lady, who was sick to the point of death to be brought to the site, and each cross in turn was placed before her to touch. On touching the first and the second she remained unmoved, but when she touched the third, she rose to her feet, pronouncing herself completely cured, thereby proving beyond all doubt to those standing by, which was the true cross.[3]

The miraculous power that lay hidden in Christian relics had been triumphantly demonstrated, and from this small beginning a great cult began to grow that was to satisfy the cravings of those who had for centuries believed in the presence of unseen spiritual power in images and all sorts of odds and ends associated with the gods. It came as a great relief to those who were even now beginning to crowd into the church from paganism and had begun to find its simple rituals rather tame, without the presence of numinous articles and images to nod at. Twenty years later, fragments of the true cross were spread over the whole world, so much so in fact, that further miraculous powers had to be evinced to explain where all the wood had come from.

Constantine himself took the cult of relics one stage further. The city of Rome possessed the bodies of the martyred apostles Peter and Paul, and they undoubtedly added great lustre to the growing status of the city, as Christian centre of the empire. His own new city of Constantinople, on the other hand, possessed none, and so, in order to remedy this defect, he had caused the relics of the apostles, Andrew, Luke and Timothy, to be transferred to churches there.[4] This disinterment and reburial of the remains of saints was in itself a quite new departure from the tradition of the church, and his example went a long way towards starting a craze for body-snatching that was to take such grotesque forms that the emperor Theodosius, some sixty years later, was driven to try to restrain the custom by law, without much success.

Bishop Ambrose of Milan, however, was to add the final touch to fan the movement into flame. He, by his style of Christian ministry was already doing more than anyone to fix the Constantinian pattern of the prince bishop on to the church for centuries to come, and now in his treatment of relics he was to follow Constantine's example to the letter, drawing out at the same time, with all his spiritual authority, its novel implications to the full.

In the summer of AD 386, Ambrose was being harassed in Milan by the empress Justina. She was a strong Arian supporter and had gathered round the court of her young son, Valentinian II, such a large Arian following that they had asked for the use of one of the catholic churches for their Easter worship, only to receive a brusque refusal from Ambrose on doctrinal grounds. The Arians were popular among the crowds for their catchy hymns and tunes, so Ambrose as a counter-blast, wrote some of the finest hymns the church possesses even to this day, to help his congregations to keep their spirits up during the long hours they were to sit in the churches to prevent the Arians from entering.

Then, as if to take the battle right into the enemy's camp, Ambrose produced a trump card. He was shown in a vision where the bodies of two Christian martyrs, Gervasius and Protasius, lay buried in the town. The bodies were dug up and taken to the basilica, named after Ambrose himself, where they were reburied amid great excitement. It was what followed that touched off the movement, for apart from anything else, the account of it was carried far and wide throughout the empire in one of the best selling books of all time, the *Confessions* of St Augustine. His description of it is very vivid;[5]

> the bodies were discovered and disinterred, and translated with fitting state to the basilica of Ambrose. And as they were borne along the road, many who were tormented by unclean spirits were healed, the very devils being constrained to make confession. Nay, there was one citizen, well known to have been blind for many years, who, when he learned the reason for that loud rejoicing, leaped up and begged his guide to lead him to the spot. It was done, and on his earnest entreaty he was allowed to touch with his hand-kerchief the bier of Thy saints, whose death is so precious in Thy sight. He laid the handkerchief on his eyes, and immediately they were opened. Hence wonder ran abroad . . .

A triumphant demonstration had been given of the numinous vibrations that lurked in Christian relics. Given enough faith they really worked, which was more than could be said of many of the old gods.

Augustine himself, for all his intellectual acumen, seems to have been completely caught up in the craze, for the relics of saints he said in Africa, not only heal the sick, they restore the dead to life, and he cites cases to prove it;[6] Paulinus of Nola too, correspondent-in-chief of the catholic Church, was quite carried away and must needs glorify his new churches with many relics of the saints placed under the altars;[7] whilst Bishop Victricius of Rouen, Martin's friend, on his return from his visit to Britain, was overcome with a near fanatical joy to discover that in his absence, Ambrose had sent him a packet of bones of the martyrs for his church. His language seems to suggest that the martyrs themselves were present in the church in the casket of bones, for he encourages the whole city to turn out to greet them on their arrival and to beg their intercession.

Martin, however, was not to be so easily carried away. He had indeed, according to Gregory,[8] whose evidence is sometimes loaded in favour of the cult, buried the body of Gatien in the church at Tours, and also received a gift of relics for the city from Milan, as Victricius had done, but he showed a healthy suspicion of the new craze. A fast-growing popular cult had sprung up near Marmoutier centred round an altar that was supposed to have been erected by former bishops of Tours in veneration of a martyr. Martin's first and typical reaction, on being told about it, was to suspect fraud. He had first demanded a clear presentation of all the facts concerning its foundation, and then visited the site in person. He then 'prayed to the Lord that He would reveal who the martyr in question was', and when the shade of a sadly penitent highwayman had appeared, he rebuked him sharply and ordered the altar to be removed.[9]

Martin, however, was dead, and bishop Brice, who had possession of his body, was not the sort of man to celebrate its arrival in Tours in a low key. In spite of Martin's known aversion to the lifestyle of Ambrose, and to many of his basic assumptions,[10] Brice was determined to give to Tours the same kind of fame that the bodies of the almost unknown Gervasius and Protasius had brought to Milan. Brice had already been accused of personal aggrandizement by spending the offerings of the faithful on 'keeping horses and purchasing slaves. . . , boys belonging to barbarous nations, and girls of a comely appearance';[11] but now his chance had at last come to capitalize on his master's fame, and through it to bring wealth and honour not only to himself but also to the city of Tours. He raised a small church over Martin's body, and people from all over Gaul started to flock there for healing. It was as if the age-old rituals of tribal journeys to the burial mounds of divine heroes or to the oracles of the gods had found a new and more heart-warming destination, with real hope that at the end something exciting might happen.

When, some forty-six years later, bishop Brice died after a somewhat unhappy and disturbed life, he was buried in the basilica beside Martin. The cult was well under way, and, as Constantine and Ambrose had clearly understood, good relics, especially those that worked, create honour not only for the individuals who possess them, but also for the towns and cities where they rest.

Brice was followed in AD 443 by bishop Eustochius, a 'pious, God-fearing man descended from a senatorial family', and he in turn was followed in AD 460 by Perpetuus; 'he, too, was of a senatorial family, or so they say, and a relative of his predecessors.'[12] Thus had begun a long line of prince bishops who were to live in a style and possess a power far in excess of anything dreamt of by any of Constantine's contemporaries. Bishop Perpetuus, 'a man of some wealth with property in quite a few cities . . . pulled down the church which bishop Bricius had earlier constructed over Saint Martin, and built another of greater size and wonderful workmanship.'[13] There was no halting the process of aggrandizement.

Monastic churches were built on the sites of Martin's humble hermitages, and elsewhere, in the surrounding countryside; pious householders built oratories on their estates and provided them with presbyters; whole Christian villages were founded, and gradually the parochial system grew, to become trapped later like a fly in aspic in the feudal system, and exported for development into Britain. The individual presbyter in his remote village was soon to be cut off by physical and spiritual distance from his bishop, and to develop into the local representative of law and order, and amateur inquisitor. It was a system of which Constantine would thoroughly have approved, but at the same time it must be confessed that, in burying Martin's body in such grandeur, they had buried the primitive church along with it, with all its vitality, intimacy, and whole-hearted dedication.

In AD 573, Gregory, the historian, a member of the rich senatorial caste from whom most bishops were then being drawn, became the nineteenth bishop of Tours. He was an ardent supporter of the cult of the saint's body and has left a vivid account of the contemporary belief in the efficacy of its numinous power. The body heals the sick, sorts out true from false oaths, settles family quarrels, provides an oracle for kings going into battle, provides a kind of sorting office for letters to the saint and is vital for the defence of the city; but underneath it all can be detected its main power, which is to enhance and act as a buttress to the authority of the bishop and his clerics.

The most famous perhaps of all the miracles at Tours occurred in AD 507 in connection with Clovis, king of the Salian Franks. The Salian Franks were a group of the invading barbarians who had settled at first in northern Gaul, and begun to extend their conquests further south. Clovis, with his army, was passing Tours on his way to do battle with Alaric II, king of the Arian Goths, who was drawn up waiting for him near Poitiers. As the army passed Tours, Gregory describes how:[14]

> In respect for St Martin, Clovis ordered that they should requisition nothing in this neighbourhood except fodder and water. One of the soldiers found some hay belonging to a poor man. 'The King commanded that nothing should be requisitioned except fodder, didn't he?' said this man. 'Well, this is fodder. We shan't be disobeying his order if we take it.' He laid hands on the poor man and took his hay by main force. This was reported to Clovis. He drew his sword and killed the soldier on the spot. 'It is no good expecting to win this fight if we offend Saint Martin', said he. This was enough to ensure that the army took nothing else from this region.

The god of the local territory, the *genius loci, Divus Martinus*,[15] had been appeased, and straightaway, conscious of his favour, Clovis sent messengers up the hill to the basilica to enquire of the saint's body an oracle concerning the imminent battle. As they entered the basilica they heard the monks chanting: 'For Thou hast girded me with strength unto the battle; Thou hast subdued under me those that rose up against me. Thou hast also given me the necks of mine enemies; that I might destroy them that hate me.' The oracle had spoken. Clovis went off towards Poitiers, defeated and slew Alaric and returned in triumph to Tours. From a most unlikely quarter a new Constantine had arisen,[16] 'In St. Martin's church he stood clad in a purple tunic and the military mantle, and he crowned himself with a Diadem.'[17]

From that moment onwards the crowds increased, flocking to Tours from far and wide. The wooden hut at Marmoutier grew into one of the richest and most famous Benedictine abbeys in the world, on whom high and low lavished gifts; even little Ligugé had its pilgrims, and all this because of the body of the *bienheureux confesseur* in his shrine on the hill at Tours.

It is clear that at every turn in the conversion of the Gallic people in these confused and cruel times, the prince bishops with remarkable shrewdness were taking full advantage of every rough and ready Constantine who might appear as an aspirant for the title of imperial protector of the church. Any of these aspiring Constantines who succeeded however, from the eighth century onwards had a new factor to contend with – the Donation of Constantine himself – whereby they found themselves very much playing second fiddle to the pope of Rome in a way that Constantine would certainly not have countenanced in his lifetime. It gradually began to dawn on everyone that the old empire, far from having sunk into oblivion, had merely changed its skin. The emperor of the West had gone, only to be replaced by the pope of Rome; the provincial governors had more or less disappeared only to be replaced by the metropolitan bishops; and the city magistrates, whilst still existing in name had to all intents and purposes been replaced by the local bishops, complete with their own courts of justice, and supported by an ever growing army of monks and parish priests, whose tentacles were reaching far into the most inaccessible places.

To prove the pope's title to this take-over, there was the 'Donation of Constantine', for all to read. In it Constantine[18]

> in gratitude for his conversion by Pope Silvester, granted to that pope and his successors for ever, not only spiritual supremacy over the other patriarchates and over all matters of faith and worship, but also of temporal dominion over Rome, Italy, and the provinces, places and civitates of the western regions.

The task of the emperor now was simply to obey the supreme pontiff by supporting his efforts to propagate Christianity and to maintain its purity; a task which meant the bringing of his military forces into action against stubborn infidels and those individuals or groups who were judged to be deviant from the strictly defined doctrines of the catholic church. It seems somehow almost incidental, in the light of the chaos of religious wars and persecutions which were to follow, that the Donation itself was proved beyond doubt to be a forgery a few hundred years later.

In spite of the gradual appearance of this mighty and all-pervasive 'City of God', the medieval church, with its two-edged sword, ready to crush all deviants; deviants there were in plenty. Many of them were inspired by the remembered dream of the glory of the primitive church, though it lay buried in Martin's tomb, along with the scriptures, now fossilized for the ordinary man, in the Latin language. The style of the primitive church was still remembered poignantly for its absolute denial of the use of the sanctions of physical violence to make or keep converts. Martin's teacher, Hilary of Poitiers, had summed it up in an open letter to the emperor Constantius II, Constantine's son: 'If force were employed to promote true religion the teaching of a bishop would go out to meet it and say: "God does not need service under stress of necessity: He does not want worship under compulsion." ' If the early church was clear on this point it was equally clear on the point that freely accepted membership of the church implied, after baptism, a total commitment; there were to be no first-, second- or third-class Christians, all travelled light, and first-class, and the destination was heaven often through the shattering experience of public humiliation and martyrdom. Martin was adamant on this point for all Christians: 'the allurements of this world and secular burdens were to be abandoned in order that we might be free and unencumbered in following the Lord Jesus.'[19]

The structure of the medieval church was built on quite different principles. It was a form of Christianity in which there had come to be recognized three quite different classes or grades of Christian piety. There were those in the first class, who lived the ascetic life, dedicated to keeping alive the spirit of primitive Christianity, holding all things in common and living in a spirit of white martyrdom – the monks and nuns and their fellow travellers. The second class embraced the ever-increasing army of clerics, of whom, though celibacy was mostly required, not such a high pitch of devotion was expected. And finally there was the great rump of the laypeople. Augustine had defined their role succinctly in rather different terms to Martin, 'a man with a few good works to his name, who slept with his wife, faute de mieux, and often just for the pleasure of it; touchy on points of honour, given to vendettas; not a landgrabber, but capable of fighting to keep hold of his own property, though only in the bishop's court; and, for all that, a good Christian, . . . "looking on himself as a disgrace, and giving the glory to God".'[20]

Lurking behind the great structure, like some vicious guard dog ready to pounce, lay the special weapons of the secular arm for dealing with deviants handed over to them by the church for treatment; torture (far more sophisticated than the noisy Romans had devised for the entertainment of the spectators in the amphitheatre), summary trial, and public death by burning. It was all done in the name of Christ, and according to the principles laid down by the blessed Augustine himself in his teaching concerning the use of *Disciplina*, or physical force to achieve conversions and maintain unity.[21]

The first Christian persecution, as an overture, had fallen on bishop Priscillian and his adherents in Spain and Gaul. His popularity had lain in that he was seeking to restore the stern ways of the church of the martyrs as the normal pattern of Christian life for everyone. As a bishop he seems to have held firmly to the Nicene faith, but he wished the church to be pure and certainly not to have in it any of Augustine's 'good laymen', or any who would go round collecting the dust off saints' tombs to carry about in a box as a charm.[22] His execution had done nothing to stop the spread of his teaching for:[23]

> After his death, not only was the heresy not suppressed, which under him as its author, had burst forth, but acquiring strength, it became more widely spread. For his followers who had previously honored him as a saint, subsequently began to honor him as a martyr.

Seven centuries later, as if from nowhere, there appeared a movement similar in many ways to that of bishop Priscillian, yet more organized and determined, and with a far larger following. Its preachers were called the *Cathari* (the pure ones), and the local people called them, *les bons hommes* or *les bons Chrétiens*; and it has been said by one who has studied them closely, that their rituals 'recall those of the primitive Church with a truth and precision the more striking, the nearer we go back to the apostolic age'.[24]

Their teaching was centred around the baptism of the spirit or *consolamentum*, which, they claimed, provided total forgiveness of sins. Those who had received this baptism became *les bons Chrétiens*, the ministers of the church, and walked on the earth as angels in human flesh. To receive the baptism of the spirit it was necessary to undergo a year's stern catechumenate, during which the candidates were called 'believers'; they fasted, prostrated themselves before their teachers as penitents, were regularly scrutinized and finally, before receiving the baptism of the spirit, the Creed and Lord's Prayer were revealed to them and their mysteries explained. They then renounced Satan as the god of this world, received the kiss of peace from the brethren, and were baptized. Kneeling before the holy table, the gospel book was taken from it and placed on their heads, the brethren meanwhile placing their hands on them as well, whilst passages about the gift of the spirit were read. At their Eucharist all the *bons Chrétiens*, men and women, went up to the table, and standing round it said the Lord's Prayer over the bread, which was then broken and handed round by the president. This much-prized, hallowed bread was reserved in a bag; some was sent to other churches as a token of fellowship, and some was kept back in order to be taken to anyone who lay dying.

The whole ritual was performed with the clear understanding that red martyrdom of a particularly cruel kind could quickly follow from the hands of the catholic church itself, and it seems as if this uncompromising conviction and hunger for spiritual fellowship with the primitive church far from discouraging converts, quickly won the movement a large following.

The first Cathars appeared around Toulouse at the beginning of the eleventh century, and in spite of repressive measures grew steadily in numbers until the common people and indeed many of the nobility over a wide area of southern France began to flock to them. By AD 1215 the matter had become so serious that pope Innocent III ordered a crusade to be mounted against them, and a devastating war followed which lasted for twenty years. When it was over the newly formed Inquisition, led by specially trained monks, moved in for the final kill, and operated unremittingly for almost two centuries, finally feeling confident that they had crushed the movement completely.

In spite of this treatment, perhaps even because of it, a similar movement had been started at Lyons by a rich merchant, Peter Waldo, who sold his goods, gave everything he had to the poor and went out as a preacher in voluntary poverty. He taught a simple gospel, and his immediate followers, like the *bons Chrétiens* were unlettered men. At first they remained faithful to the baptism and communion of the catholic Church, but were so hounded and persecuted that they fled for refuge into the mountains, eventually settling in the Alpine valleys to the south west of Turin, one of which significantly they named after St Martin. Here to this day their descendants live out their religion, a most venerable link of Protestantism with the Christians of earlier centuries.

Throughout history Martin has kept a foot in all Christian camps. Revered by the catholic Church of Gaul at the tomb in Tours, and in thousands of churches dedicated in his name throughout the world, cherished in the Celtic monasteries, and yet at home with the refugees in the Waldensian valleys; he is an apostle of the Catholic Church and yet in a way the founding father of Protestantism. Much water has flowed under the bridges of Tours since that first day in AD 370, when he was led across, an unwilling victim to take up his ministry in the town. Now on the site of bishop Brice's little church, stands a great basilica, still visited by pilgrims from all over the world. In a shrine on the original spot, lies a piece of the saint's body still, and faithful Christians gather in veneration beside it to celebrate Eucharist, just as they did in the catacombs by the tombs of the martyrs.

But times have changed – the glorious dream of Constantine fades and Augustine's reasoning about the use of physical force to encourage and maintain Christian faith and unity is gradually being forgotten, though it lies buried deep in the subconscious minds of Christians. With the passing of such 'sanctions', the churches shrink in numbers, especially those that were established, but some wholesome results are following. Everywhere throughout the Christian world, as if led by the Spirit, Christians are going back to their roots again. It is not ' "Primitivism", the conviction that to find the authentic church

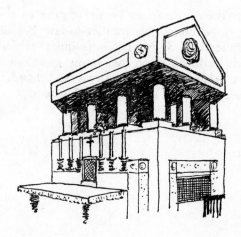

12 *Tomb of St Martin*

we must go back to the first century . . .'[25] and then childishly try to recreate some romantic illusion of what seems an ideal age. Rather it is as if the thought of those first ages, and their priorities, helps Christians to sort out in the light of many new insights from other disciplines, the elements in their denominational stances that are of lasting relevance and those which are ephemeral and stultifying.

A notable example of this frame of mind was given when a dignitary of the Roman Catholic Church was describing his arrival in France in 1945:[26]

> I have personally and for many years had a great devotion to St Martin. Since the days when I was a student – as a young priest, then as a teacher of patristics at the Lateran – I have always longed to know more of this great saint. I wanted from the first months of my arrival in France as Papal Nuncio, to go to pray at his tomb and to venerate at Candes the places sanctified by his death. In memory of this double visit, I caused to be placed in the crypt of the famous sanctuary at Tours the following inscription:
>
> Angelus Joseph Roncalli, Bergomas, Apostolic Nunce in Gaul, client of St Martin, the humble man of Tours. Blessed Martin preserve the clergy and people of Gaul. Look after your own everywhere.

Ten years later the writer was to become pope John XXIII, and suddenly and quite unexpectedly in the basilica of St Paul in Rome, as if he had been illuminated by a flash of heavenly light, to call into being the Second Vatican Council, from which so much original and creative Christian work in all the churches is still growing.

Sulpitius Severus, as he drew near to the end of the descriptive letter he wrote to his mother-in-law Bassula, concerning the death and funeral of St Martin, was quite carried away and ended thus: 'I trust he looks upon me, as my guardian while I am writing these things, and upon you while you read them'.

It seems a good note on which to end.

Notes

CHAPTER I

1 Gregory of Tours, *History of the Franks*, trans. Lewis Thorpe, Harmondsworth, Penguin, 1974, II:1.
2 Paulinus of Nola, *Letters of Paulinus of Nola*, trans. P. G. Walsh, London, Longmans Green, 1967, letter 5:4, p. 56.
3 Ibid., Introduction, p. 2.
4 Ibid., letter 5:5, pp. 56ff.
5 e.g. 'Severus, Sulpicius', *Encyclopaedia Britannica*, Edition XI, New York, 1910–11, volume xxiv, p. 726.
6 Sulpitius Severus, *Works of Sulpitius Severus*, trans. Alexander Roberts, Library of the Nicene and Post-Nicene Fathers of the Christian Church, Oxford, James Parker, 1894, volume XI, *Life of St Martin*, chapter xxv.
7 Paulinus of Nola, letter 35.
8 Sulpitius Severus, letter III.
9 Paulinus of Nola, letter 11, p. 101.
10 Sulpitius Severus, *Dialogues*, I, chapter xxiii.
11 H. Mayr-Harting, *The Coming of Christianity to Anglo-Saxon England*, London, Batsford, 1972, pp. 86–7.
12 Sulpitius Severus, p. 18.
13 Stuart Piggott, *The Druids*, London, Thames & Hudson, 1968; Anne Ross, *Everyday Life of the Pagan Celts*, London, Batsford, 1970.
14 Sulpitius Severus, *Sacred History*, book II:41.
15 Ibid., book I:1.

CHAPTER 2

1 Sulpitius Severus, *Works of Sulpitius Severus*, trans. Alexander Roberts, Library of the Nicene and Post-Nicene Fathers of the Christian Church, Oxford, James Parker, 1894, volume XI, *Life of St Martin*, chapter ii.
2 See the discussion about dating in Jacques Fontaine, 'Verité et fiction dans la chronologie de la vita Martini', *Saint Martin et son temps*, Studia Anselmiana, no. 46, Rome, Herder, 1961, p. 189.

3 Michael Grant, *The Climax of Rome*, London, Weidenfeld & Nicolson, 1968, pp. 7 and 15.

4 Ibid., p. 7.

5 Ibid., p. 237.

6 'Forty Martyrs of Sebastia', *Butler's Lives of the Saints*, ed. Herbert Thurston and Donald Attwater, London, Burns & Oates, 1956, volume I, 10 March, p. 541.

7 Lecoy de la Marche, *Saint Martin*, Tours, Alfred Mame et fils, 1881, p. 73.

8 Sulpitius Severus, *Life of St Martin*, chapter ii.

9 Tertullian, *Treatises concerning Prayer, concerning Baptism*, trans. Alexander Souter, London, SPCK, 1919, p. 68.

10 W. K. Lowther Clarke, *Liturgy and Worship*, London, SPCK, 1932; W. Smith and S. Cheetham, eds, *Dictionary of Christian Antiquities*, London, John Murray, 1875, articles on Baptism and Catechumens.

11 Sulpitius Severus, *Life of St Martin*, chapter ii.

CHAPTER 3

1 Jacques Fontaine, 'Verité et fiction dans la chronologie de la vita Martini,' *Saint Martin et son temps*, Studia Anselmiana no. 46, Rome, Herder, 1961, p. 200.

2 Sulpitius Severus, *Works of Sulpitius Severus*, trans. Alexander Roberts, Library of the Nicene and Post-Nicene Fathers of the Christian Church, London, James Parker, 1894, volume XI, *Life of St Martin*, chapter ii.

3 Donald Dudley, *Roman Society*, London, Penguin, 1970, p. 166.

4 William Whiston, *The Works of Flavius Josephus*, Edinburgh, William P. Nimmo, not dated, book III: v, p. 505.

5 G. R. Watson, *Training and the Life of a Roman Soldier*, London, Thames & Hudson, 1970.

6 Lecoy de la Marche, *Saint Martin*, Tours, Alfred Mame et fils, 1881, p. 87.

7 Sulpitius Severus, *Life of St Martin*, chapter ii.

8 Ibid., chapter iii.

9 For references to the primitive catechumenate and baptism, see: W. K. Lowther Clarke, *Liturgy and Worship*, London, SPCK, 1932, pp. 410ff; L. Duchesne, *Christian Worship its Origin and Evolution*, London, SPCK, 1904, pp. 299ff; Peter Brown, *St Augustine of Hippo*, London, Faber & Faber, 1969; B. J. Kidd, ed., *Documents Illustrative of the History of the Church*, London, SPCK, 1938, volume II, no. 171.

10 John Scarborough, *Roman Medicine*, London, Thames & Hudson, 1969, pp. 66ff.

11 Second Epistle to Timothy, 2:3.

12 L. Duchesne, *Early History of the Christian Church*, London, John Murray, 1914, volume II, pp. 394ff.

CHAPTER 4

1 T. Scott Holmes, *The Christian Church in Gaul*, London, Macmillan, 1911, pp. 105–6.

2 W. Smith and S. Cheetham, eds, *Dictionary of Christian Antiquities*, London, John Murray, 1875, article on money.

3 B. J. Kidd, ed., *Documents Illustrative of the History of the Church*, London, SPCK, 1938, volume I, p. 234.

4 Ibid., volume I, p. 5.

5 Ibid., volume I, p. 75.

6 Jacob Burckhardt, *The Age of Constantine*, trans. Moses Hadas, London, Routledge & Kegan Paul, 1949, p. 307.

7 L. Duchesne, *Early History of the Christian Church*, London, John Murray, 1914, volume II, p. 95.

8 A. P. Stanley, *History of the Eastern Church*, London, John Murray, 1894, p. 93.

9 Camille Jullian, *Histoire des Gaules*, Paris, 1927, book 7, p. 160.

10 Duchesne, op. cit., volume II, chapter 8, p. 248.

11 Kidd, ed., op. cit., volume II, p. 202.

12 K. S. Painter, 'A Roman silver treasure from Canterbury', *Journal of the Archaeological Association*, third series, volume xxviii, 1965, pp. 3ff.

13 Sulpitius Severus, *Works of Sulpitius Severus*, trans. Alexander Roberts, Library of the Nicene and Post-Nicene Fathers of the Christian Church, Oxford, James Parker, 1894, volume XI, *Life of St Martin*, chapter iv.

14 Duchesne, op. cit., volume II, pp. 258ff.

15 Stuart Piggott, *The Druids*, London, Thames & Hudson, 1968, pp. 197ff.

CHAPTER 5

1 Sulpitius Severus, *Works of Sulpitius Severus*, trans. Alexander Roberts, Library of the Nicene and Post-Nicene Fathers of the Christian Church, Oxford, James Parker, 1894, volume XI, *Life of St Martin*, chapter v.

2 St Ambrose, *Some of the Principal Works of St. Ambrose*, trans. H. de Romestin, Library of the Nicene and Post-Nicene Fathers of the Christian Church, Oxford, James Parker, 1896, volume X, epistle lxiii, 66–71.

3 T. Scott Holmes, *The Christian Church in Gaul*, London, Macmillan, 1911, pp. 177–8.

4 Sulpitius Severus, *Vie de St Martin*, introduction, text and translation by Jacques Fontaine, *Sources Chrétiennes*, Paris, Les Editions du Cerf, 1967, chapter v; latin text, '*temptavit autem idem Hilarius imposito diaconatus officio sibi eum artius inplicare et ministerio uincere diuino.*'

5 *Seven Ecumenical Councils of the Undivided Church*, trans. and ed. Henry Percival, Library of the Nicene and Post-Nicene Fathers of the Christian Church, London, James Parker, 1894, volume XIV, p. 423, excursus on canon ix of the Council of Sardica.

6 *Apostolic Constitutions*, trans. A. Roberts and J. Donaldson, Ante-Nicene Christian Library, Edinburgh, T. & T. Clark, 1870, volume XVII, viii:26

7 Sulpitius Severus, *Life of St Martin*, chapter v.

8 Gregory of Tours, *History of the Franks*, trans. Lewis Thorpe, Harmondsworth, Penguin, 1974, II:1, p. 104.

9 Sulpitius Severus, *Dialogues*, II, chapters ix and x.

10 *Seven Ecumenical Councils of the Undivided Church*, Council of Antioch in Encaenis, AD 341, canons viii and ix, p. 112.

11 Sulpitius Severus, *Life of St Martin*, chapter v.

12 Ibid., chapter vi.

13 Homer, *Iliad*, trans. E. V. Rieu, Harmondsworth, Penguin, 1969.

14 L. Duchesne, *Early History of the Christian Church*, London, John Murray, 1914, volume II, p. 287.

15 Peter Brown, *St. Augustine of Hippo*, London, Faber, 1969, p. 71; H. V. Morton, *A Traveller in Italy*, London, Methuen, 1964.

16 B. J. Kidd, ed., *Documents Illustrative of the History of the Church*, London, SPCK, 1938, volume II, p. 135.

17 F. Homes Dudden, *Life and Times of St Ambrose*, Oxford, Clarendon Press, 1935, volume I, p. 65 (note 3).

18 St Augustine, *The Confessions of St. Augustine*, trans. C. Bigg, London, Methuen, 1907, book viii, chapter vi.

19 Sulpitius Severus, *Life of St Martin*, chapter vi.

20 Sulpitius Severus, *Sacred History*, chapter xli.

CHAPTER 6

1 Helen Waddell, *The Desert Fathers*, London, Constable, 1936, p. 36.

2 Søren Kierkegaard, *The Journals of Kierkegaard, 1834–1854*, London, Collins (Fontana), 1958, p. 185.

3 Waddell, op. cit., p. 43.

4 St Athanasius, *Life of St. Anthony*, trans. H. Ellershaw, Library of the Nicene and Post-Nicene Father of the Christian Church, volume IV, Oxford, James Parker, 1892,

5 'Hellebore', *Encyclopaedia Britannica*, edition XI, New York, 1910–11, volume xiii, p. 235.

CHAPTER 7

1 Dom. Jean Coquet OSB, *L'Interêt des fouilles de Ligugé*, Ligugé, Société des Amis du vieux Ligugé, 1960.

2 Sulpitius Severus, *Works of Sulpitius Severus*, trans. Alexander Roberts, Library of the Nicene and Post-Nicene Fathers of the Christian Church, Oxford, James Parker, 1894, volume XI, *Life of St Martin*, chapter vii.

3 Ibid.

4 Epistle to the Romans, 8:23.

5 First Book of Kings, 18, and Second Book of Kings, 2, 3, etc.
6 Epistle to the Hebrews, 2:14.
7 Yves Bordonneau, 'La morte resusscitée', Poitiers, *Si Poitiers*, p. 57.
8 Second Book of Kings, 4:33ff.
9 Gregory of Tours, *History of the Franks*, trans. Lewis Thorpe, Harmondsworth, Penguin, 1974, I:48, p. 98.
10 Coquet, op. cit.
11 Sulpitius Severus, *Life of St Martin*, chapter viii.

CHAPTER 8

1 Sulpitius Severus, *Works of Sulpitius Severus*, trans. Alexander Roberts, Library of the Nicene and Post-Nicene Fathers of the Christian Church, Oxford, James Parker, 1894, volume XI, *Life of St Martin*, chapter vii.
2 J. B. Lightfoot, *The Two Epistles of Clement to the Corinthians*, London, Macmillan, 1869, p. 137.
3 First Epistle of St Peter, 2:4 and 9.
4 W. Smith and S. Cheetham, eds, *Dictionary of Christian Antiquities*, London, John Murray, 1875, article on Election; also, 'excursus on canon iv of the council of Nicaea' in *Seven Ecumenical Councils of the Undivided Church*, trans. and ed. Henry Percival, Library of the Nicene and Post-Nicene Fathers of the Christian Church, London, James Parker, 1894, volume XIV.
5 Smith and Cheetham, eds, op. cit., p. 215.
6 Jean Gaudemet, *L'Église dans l'Empire Romain, IVe et Ve siècles*, Paris, Siray, 1958, p. 167.
7 Lecoy de la Marche, *St Martin*, Tours, Alfred Mame et fils, 1881, pp. 178–9.
8 *Encyclopaedia Britannica*, edition XI, New York, 1910–11, volume 8, p. 597, article on Druidism: 'Ausonius, for instance, apostrophizes the rhetorician Attius Pater as sprung from a race of Druids.'
9 Peter Brown, *St. Augustine of Hippo*, London, Faber & Faber, 1969, p. 138, sermon 355.2.
10 Sulpitius Severus, *Life of St Martin*, chapter ix.
11 B. J. Kidd, ed., *Documents Illustrative of the History of the Church*, London, SPCK, 1938, volume II, no. 192, p. 250.
12 Paulinus of Nola, *Letters of Paulinus of Nola*, trans. P. G. Walsh, London, Longmans Green, 1967, letter 22.
13 Ibid.
14 Brown, op. cit., p. 138.
15 Sulpitius Severus, *Dialogues*, III, chapter x.

CHAPTER 9

1 W. Smith and S. Cheetham, eds, *Dictionary of Christian Antiquities*, London, John Murray, 1875, article on Secretarium.

2 Gregory of Tours, *History of the Franks*, trans. Lewis Thorpe, Harmondsworth, Penguin, 1974, introduction, pp. 9–13.

3 John Cassian, *Conferences*, trans. Edgar Gibson, Library of the Nicene and Post-Nicene Father of the Christian Church, Oxford, James Parker, 1894, volume XI, 'First conference of Abbot Theonas', p. 515.

4 Stuart Piggott, *The Druids*, London, Thames & Hudson, 1968, p. 113.

5 Sulpitius Severus, *Works of Sulpitius Severus*, trans. Alexander Roberts, Library of the Nicene and Post-Nicene Fathers of the Christian Church, Oxford, James Parker, 1894, volume XI, *Life of St Martin*, chapter x; W. Douglas Simpson, *Saint Ninian and the origins of the Christian Church in Scotland*, Edinburgh, Oliver & Boyd, 1940, pp. 37ff.

6 Acts of the Apostles, 6.

7 Sulpitius Severus, *Dialogues*, II, chapter xiv.

8 Ibid., *Dialogues*, III, chapter x.

9 Ibid., *Life of St Martin*, chapter xxi.

10 Ibid., *Dialogues*, III, chapter xiv.

11 Ibid., *Dialogues*, II, chapter xi.

12 Lord David Cecil, *Visionary and Dreamer*, London, Constable, 1969, p. 56.

13 Sulpitius Severus, *Dialogues*, III, chapter xiv.

14 Helen Waddell, *The Desert Fathers*, London, Constable, 1936.

15 Second Epistle to Timothy, 2:4.

16 Sulpitius Severus, *Life of St Martin*, chapter x.

17 Ibid., chapter xxvi.

18 Ibid., *Dialogues*, II, chapter i.

19 Robert Payne, *The Life and Death of Mahatma Gandhi*, London, Bodley Head, 1969, p. 294.

CHAPTER 10

1 Gaston Dahl, *Picasso*, Lugano, Uffici Press, no date, p. 28.

2 John Cassian, *Conferences*, trans. Edgar Gibson, Library of the Nicene and Post-Nicene Fathers of the Christian Church, Oxford, James Parker, 1894, volume XI, 'First conference of Abbot Moses', chapter vii.

3 Ibid., chapter xv.

4 Sulpitius Severus, *Works of Sulpitius Severus*, trans. Alexander Roberts, Library of the Nicene and Post-Nicene Fathers of the Christian Church, Oxford, James Parker, 1894, volume XI, *Life of St Martin*, chapter xxvi.

5 Sulpitius Severus, *Dialogues*, II, chapter xiii.

6 Mona Wilson, *Life of William Blake*, Oxford University Press, London, 1971, pp. 309ff.

7 Mary the harlot, for whose story, see: Helen Waddell, *The Desert Fathers*, London, Constable, 1936, pp. 303ff; *Memorial de l' Année Martinienne*, Libraire Philosophique, Paris, J. Vrin, 1962, p. 3, note.

8 *Butler's Lives of the Saints*, ed. Herbert Thurston and Donald Attwater, London, Burns & Oates, 1956, volume III, 23 September, p. 623, 'Thecla'.

9 B. J. Kidd, ed., *Documents Illustrative of the History of the Church*, London, SPCK, 1920, volume I, no. 42, p. 75.

10 Sulpitius Severus, *Dialogues*, II, chapter ii, and III, chapter x.

11 Sulpitius Severus, *Life of St Martin*, chapter xxi.

12 Wilson, op. cit., p. 73.

13 First Epistle to the Corinthians, 12:10.

14 T. Scott Holmes, *The Christian Church in Gaul*, London, Macmillan, 1911, p. 176.

15 Sulpitius Severus, *Life of St Martin*, chapter xxiv.

16 Jacob Burckhardt, *The Age of Constantine*, trans. Moses Hadas, London, Routledge & Kegan Paul, 1949, p. 195.

17 Sulpitius Severus, *Life of St Martin*, chapter xxv.

CHAPTER 11

1 Sulpitius Severus, *Works of Sulpitius Severus*, trans. Alexander Roberts, Library of the Nicene and Post-Nicene Fathers of the Christian Church, Oxford, James Parker, 1894, volume XI, *Life of St Martin*, chapter xix.

2 Gospel according to St Mark, 3:22; Gospel according to St Luke, 13:16.

3 *Encyclopaedia Britannica*, edition XI, New York, 1910–11, volume xviii, p. 45, article on Medicine.

4 John Scarborough, *Roman Medicine*, London, Thames & Hudson, 1969, pp. 66ff.

5 Gospel according to St Mark, 6:13.

6 Epistle of St James, 5:13ff.

7 W. Smith and S. Cheetham, eds, *Dictionary of Christian Antiquities*, London, John Murray, 1875, article on Unction, p. 2004.

8 L. Duchesne, *Christian Worship*, trans. C. Donaldson, London, SPCK, 1904, p. 306.

9 Sulpitius Severus, *Dialogues*, III, chapter iii.

10 W. K. Lowther Clarke, ed., *Liturgy and Worship*, London, SPCK, 1932, p. 483.

11 Sulpitius Severus, *Dialogues*, II, chapter ii.

12 Lowther Clarke, op. cit., p. 495.

13 Smith and Cheetham, op. cit., article on Demoniacs, p. 544.

14 Sulpitius Severus, *Dialogues*, III, chapter vi.

CHAPTER 12

1 Sulpitius Severus, *Works of Sulpitius Severus*, trans. Alexander Roberts, Library of the Nicene and Post-Nicene Fathers of the Christian Church Oxford, James Parker, 1894, volume XI, *Life of St Martin*, chapter xiv.

2 Bullfinch, *Mythology*, London, Spring Books, 1964, p. 39.

3 L. Duchesne, *Early History of the Christian Church*, London, John Murray, 1912, volume I, chapter i.

4 Anne Ross, *Everyday Life of the Pagan Celts*, London, Batsford, 1974, p. 183.

5 Stuart Piggott, *The Druids*, London, Thames & Hudson, 1968, p. 120.

6 Jacob Burckhardt, *The Age of Constantine*, trans. Moses Hadas, London, Routledge & Kegan Paul, 1949, p. 41.

7 Piggott, op. cit., p. 213.

8 See Chapter 8, note 8.

9 Duchesne, op. cit., volume II, p. 29.

10 Ibid., p. 60.

11 W. Smith and S. Cheetham, eds, *Dictionary of Christian Antiquities*, London, John Murray, 1875, article on Paganism, p. 1538; Duchesne, op. cit., volume II, pp. 496ff.

12 Libanius, *Selected Works*, ed. A. F. Norman, Loeb Classical Library, London, Heinemann, 1927, oration xxx: 8, volume II, p. 107, translated from the Latin text by C. Donaldson.

13 First Book of Kings, 18; Second Book of Kings, 9, and 10:27.

14 Sulpitius Severus, *Life of St Martin*, chapter xiv.

15 Lecoy de la Marche, *Saint Martin*, Tours, Alfred Mame et fils, 1881, p. 309; Sulpitius Severus, *Life of St Martin*, chapter xiii.

16 John Ferguson, *Religions of the Roman Empire*, London, Thames & Hudson, 1970, p. 26.

17 Sulpitius Severus, *Dialogues*, II, chapter iii.

CHAPTER 13

1 L. Duchesne, *Early History of the Christian Church*, London, John Murray, 1912, volume II, p. 371.

2 Peter Brown, *St. Augustine of Hippo*, London, Faber & Faber, 1969, pp. 235ff.

3 Sulpitius Severus, *Works of Sulpitius Severus*, trans. Alexander Roberts, Library of the Nicene and Post-Nicene Fathers of the Christian Church, Oxford, James Parker, 1894, volume XI, *Sacred History*, book II, chapter xlvi.

4 Duchesne, op. cit., volume II, p. 422.

5 Sulpitius Severus, *Dialogues*, II, chapter vi.

6 Sulpitius Severus, *Sacred History*, book II, chapter l.

7 Sulpitius Severus, *Life of St Martin*, chapter xx.

8 Sulpitius Severus, *Sacred History*, book II, chapter li.

9 Sulpitius Severus, *Dialogues*, II, chapters vi and vii.

10 Ibid., III, chapter xiii.

11 Ibid., III, chapter xiii.

12 B. J. Kidd, ed., *Documents Illustrative of the History of the Church*, London, SPCK, 1938, volume II, no. 85, p. 112.

13 Ibid., no. 69, p. 97.

CHAPTER 14

1 G. W. O. Addleshaw, *The Beginnings of the Parochial System*, London, St Anthony's Press, no date, no. 3, p. 5.
2 *Seven Ecumenical Councils of the Undivided Church*, trans. and ed. Henry Percival, Library of the Nicene and Post-Nicene Fathers of the Christian Church, London, James Parker, 1894, volume XIV, 'Council of Sardica', canons vi and xii.
3 Sulpitius Severus, *Works of Sulpitius Severus*, trans. Alexander Roberts, Library of the Nicene and Post-Nicene Fathers of the Christian Church, Oxford, James Parker, 1894, volume XI, *Dialogues*, III, chapter viii.
4 Gregory of Tours, *History of the Franks*, trans. Lewis Thorpe, Harmondsworth, Penguin, 1974, X:31, p. 595.
5 See local guide books at Amboise and Candes for details.
6 W. Smith and S. Cheetham, eds, *Dictionary of Christian Antiquities*, London, John Murray, 1875, article on Chorepiscopus; and *Seven Ecumenical Councils of the Undivided Church*, volume XIV, excursus on 'Chorepiscopus', p. 21.
7 Sulpitius Severus, letter I.
8 Sulpitius Severus, *Dialogues*, II, chapter ix.
9 Sulpitius Severus, letter I.
10 Sulpitius Severus, *Dialogues*, II, chapter xiv.
11 Sulpitius Severus, *Life of St Martin*, chapter xxvii.
12 Sulpitius Severus, letter III.
13 Sulpitius Severus, *Dialogues*, III, chapter xv.
14 J. Fontaine, 'Verité et fiction dans la chronologie de la vita Martini', *Saint Martin et son temps*, Studia Anselmiana, no. 46, Rome, Herder, 1961, p. 213.
15 Sulpitius Severus, letter III.
16 '*Nullam renego laborem.*'
17 T. S. Eliot, 'Little Gidding', *Four Quartets*, London, Faber & Faber, 1959, p. 51.

CHAPTER 15

1 Gregory of Tours, *History of the Franks*, trans. Lewis Thorpe, Harmondsworth, Penguin, 1974, I:48.
2 Sulpitius Severus, *Works of Sulpitius Severus*, trans. Alexander Roberts, Library of the Nicene and Post-Nicene Fathers, of the Christian Church, Oxford, James Parker, 1894, volume XI, letter III.
3 T. Scott Holmes, *The Christian Church in Gaul*, London, Macmillan, 1911, p. 281.
4 Stuart Piggott, *The Druids*, London, Thames & Hudson, 1968, p. 113.
5 Sheppard Frere, *Britannia*, London, Routledge & Kegan Paul, 1967, plate 13.
6 Sulpitius Severus, *Dialogues*, II, chapter vi.

7 Edmund Bishop, 'Victricius, an episode in the history of the British Church', *Downside Review*, 1895, p. 12; and Sulpitius Severus, *Dialogues*, III, chapter ii.

8 Bede, *Ecclesiastical History of England*, trans. and ed. J. A. Giles, London, George Bell, 1894, book III, chapter iv.

9 Ibid., book I, chapters xxv and xxvi, pp. 38, 39.

10 C. F. Routledge, *St Martin's Church, Canterbury*, London, Kegan Paul, Trench & Trubner, 1891.

11 Kenneth Painter, 'A Roman silver treasure from Canterbury', *Journal of the Archaeological Association*, third series, volume xxviii, 1965.

12 G. W. Meates, *Lullingstone Roman Villa, Kent*, London, HMSO, 1969.

13 Cp. Sulpitius Severus, *Dialogues*, III, chapter viii.

14 Society of Antiquaries, *Report of Research Committee, no. xii, Maiden Castle*, London, Oxford University Press, 1943.

15 Sulpitius Severus, *Life of St Martin*, chapter xiii.

16 H. Mayr-Harting, *The Coming of Christianity to Anglo-Saxon England*, London, Batsford, 1972.

17 E. A. Cooke, *St Columba*, Simpkins Marshall, 1888, pp. 35 and 46; and Lucy Menzies, *St. Columba of Iona*, Iona, The Iona Community, 1949.

18 Ibid., p. 96.

19 Ibid., p. 22.

CHAPTER 16

1 Sir Kenneth Clark, *Civilization*, London, BBC and John Murray, 1969, pp. 6–7.

2 Gregory of Tours, *History of the Franks*, trans. Lewis Thorpe, Harmondsworth, Penguin, 1974, X:31.

3 Sulpitius Severus, *Works of Sulpitius Severus*, trans. Alexander Roberts, Library of the Nicene and Post-Nicene Fathers of the Christian Church, Oxford, James Parker, 1894, volume XI, *Sacred History*, book II, chapter xxxiv.

4 W. Smith and S. Cheetham, eds, *Dictionary of Christian Antiquities*, London, John Murray, 1875, article on Relics, p. 1771.

5 St Augustine, *Confessions of St. Augustine*, trans. C. Bigg, London, Methuen, 1897, book IX, chapter viii, p. 312.

6 Peter Brown, *St. Augustine of Hippo*, London, Faber & Faber, 1969, p. 417, *De Civitate Dei*, xxii:8:12.

7 Paulinus of Nola, *Letters of Paulinus of Nola*, trans. P. G. Walsh, London, Longmans Green, 1967, letter 32.

8 Edmund Bishop, 'Victricius, an episode in the History of the British Church', *Downside Review*, 1895, de laude Sanctorum.

9 Sulpitius Severus, *Life of St Martin*, chapter xi.

10 Sulpitius Severus, *Dialogues*, I, chapter xxv.

11 Ibid., III, chapter xv.

12 Gregory of Tours, X:31.

13 Ibid.

14 Ibid., II:37.

15 Lecoy de la Marche, *Saint Martin*, Tours, Alfred Mame et fils, 1881, p. 488, inscription found on a vase in Vendée.

16 Gregory of Tours, II:31.

17 Ibid., II:38.

18 *Encyclopaedia Britannica*, edition XI, New York, 1910–11, volume 8, p. 409, article on Donation of Constantine.

19 Sulpitius Severus, *Life of St Martin*, chapter xxv.

20 Brown, op. cit., pp. 233ff.

21 Ibid., p. 348.

22 Gregory of Tours, VIII:15.

23 Sulpitius Severus, *Sacred History*, book II, chapter li.

24 *Encyclopaedia Britannica*, volume 5, p. 575, article on Cathars.

25 M. Ramsey and L. J. Suenens, *The Future of the Christian Church*, London, SCM Press, 1971, p. 78.

26 Pope John XXIII, 'Lettre a son Excellence Mgr. Ferrand, en date, 10 Decembre, 1960', quoted from the *Memorial de l'Année Martinienne*, Libraire Philosophique, Paris, J. Vrin, 1962, trans. C. Donaldson.

Index